CATHLINE MARAMBAKUYANA

Unlocking Your Miracles Through Working Talents

Copyright © 2019 by Cathline Marambakuyana

All rights reserved. No part of this publication may be reproduced, stored or transmitted in any form or by any means, electronic, mechanical, photocopying, recording, scanning, or otherwise without written permission from the publisher. It is illegal to copy this book, post it to a website, or distribute it by any other means without permission.

First edition

*This book was professionally typeset on Reedsy.
Find out more at reedsy.com*

Contents

Foreword iv
Acknowledgement v
Dedication vii
Introduction ix
1. My Background 1
2. A Training School 7
3. A Willing Heart 12
4. Confession of Faith! 18
5. Spirit of Joy As We Work Talents 26
6. Talents Rounds (Money Clubs) 35
7. Good Godly Pressure When Working Talents 44
8. Monthly Big Days- Appreciation 52
9. Some Suggestions of Things We Can Do To Work Talents 59
10. Testimonies of Miracles After Working Talents 70
Conclusion 107

Foreword

Cathrine Marurama is a woman who lives what she teaches (preaches). This is not just an ordinary book, but it's a practical book, where Cathrine is sharing her teachings and her life in a testimonial book. She has done outstanding teaching on Giving and on working Talents.

Cathrine is a gifted woman in teaching on Giving, and whenever she teaches people respond because she teaches what she lives. She is an Evangelist. When it comes to teaching in the area of Giving or working Talents in our church, she is Number One. We depend on her and we send her to areas where people do not practice giving, so she can revive them.

If anyone reads this book and do what she says in her book, you will have it, because she has been doing it herself. She was an ordinary woman and God began to use her in the area of Giving and working Talents.

I want to repeat again, it's a true book, a real book. She teaches what she practices, and this book will transform the lives of many.

-Apostle Ezekiel H. Guti

Acknowledgement

I would like to acknowledge my husband, the man of God in my life for always being there for me, standing with me and supporting me in my Ministry. All my giving is made possible by my husband because he allows me to give God, he understands my passion for giving and he makes it possible for me to give.

My children, Diana Blessing, Elshina, Natasha and Tatenda you are my immediate support and encouragement. Thank you for your support and encouragement always.

Pheim Guti for helping me and advising me to use One Note to write books. It has made my life so easy and has helped me to type this book in a short time. God bless you Son.

Steve-Tharreo Simukai, for the cover of the book, typesetting and submitting to publishers. You are such a blessing. Thank you for your patience and professionalism. You ignited the fire to write books that was in me because it was not so difficult after I started working with you. May the Lord bless you and give you more clients in this area.

Overseer Molly Muzanamombe for proof reading this book and making some spelling and grammar corrections. God bless you.

Last but not least, God the father, Jesus my Saviour and the Holy Spirit for inspiring me as I wrote this book. I could feel your presence as I was writing. You are worthy to receive all the Glory for this book

Dedication

I would like to dedicate this book to the Ruwa church Zimbabwe, Wellington church New Zealand, Christ Church Forward in faith New Zealand, Dallas church USA and Boston church USA for the zeal and excitement you showed in working talents when we were your pastors. This book has become possible because of all the testimonies that I could not keep to myself.

Ruwa church, 20 March 2005,on our last Talents big day before we went to New Zealand, you raised 223 million dollars(equivalent to 223 thousand US dollars now or more) in one day. That was God, the Lord used you to motivate others.

Wellington church, you were the first church that God used in New Zealand to make the New Zealand dollar cheap. By working those 2005 Talents you motivated the other churches and showed them big amounts of money can be given to God. That time people used to say $20 is a lot of money here, but after giving big in Talents people made the NZ dollar cheap.

Christchurch you were number one when we worked towards our National Centre in New Zealand and you excelled in the area of **giving**. The highest amount we raised for talents in one day was Seventy-Six Thousand dollars and we raised a total of $450 thousand dollars towards talents that yer. That was awesome. You demonstrated a true spirit of giving in every way. Individuals giving a thousand dollars or more became a very common occurance in our services.

Dallas church you made a big impact when we raised One Hundred Thousand dollars in one day. You also worked outstandingly when we started working towards our Centre. Keep up the good work.

Boston church you made me proud, being a baby church. We started working talents 4 months after Apostle E.H. Guti planted the church and we excelled. You were number one in the whole nation, Forward in Faith church. You motivated others.

I would also want to dedicate this book to Elder Sizani Mhlanga and Elder Violet Gonzo, these two always pull others up because of their consistence in the area of **giving**, they are outstanding Big Givers in our church in the USA and I believe soon they will lead in Forward In Faith as a whole.

It would also be unfair to talk about Talents and Giving in the USA and leave out names like Pastors Dumi and Coleen Mawoyo, Elders Derek and Tanaka Shonhiwa and Elder Sam and Lizzie Mtizwa, and all those whose testimonies on working Talents I have included in this book. There are many others but these few are outstanding.

My father and mother Apostles Ezekiel and Eunor Guti, your example in the area of Giving and working Talents have brought us, as a church, this far.

Introduction

Mathew 25 vs 14-30

The concept and idea of Talents was derived from the above scripture(parable) which talks about productivity or fruitfulness. After we have been saved, Our master Jesus Christ expects us to be useful and to use our talents that God has given us to expand the Kingdom of God financially.

This kind of productivity is not equal , but our master expects productivity and fruitfulness according to the ability that God has given us. Talents is whereby we use our ability, our skill, our profession, our wisdom in business to make money and bring it to the House of the Lord. It is the means to raise money for big church projects like buying church vehicles, building church buildings, hospitals and universities.

It is one way of working for the Lord where no one should say or can say , "I do not have the money" because it is what I do that will bring about the money , that was initially not there. Actually, many people are surprised at the amount of money they manage to raise when they willingly work Talents. In most cases it's the kind of money they never imagined they could ever give to the Lord in a stipulated time. It has made us to conclude therefore that Talents are of God and that people are channels that God uses to bring money into God's church.

The most and foremost qualification to work Talents is a willing heart.

"Speak to the children of Israel, that they bring Me an offering. From everyone who gives it willingly with his heart you shall take My offering."
   Exodus 25:2 NKJV

In our church Forward In Faith Ministries International, it is the pattern and the Vision that our Archbishop Apostle E. H. Guti was given by God as a way to run a debt free church, which of course will produce debt free believers, and not only that but it is the shortest route to deliver people from spirit of poverty and joyfully usher them from poverty to prosperity.

"Give, and it will be given to you: good measure, pressed down, shaken together, and running over will be put into your bosom. For with the same measure that you use, it will be measured back to you."
   Luke 6:38 NKJV

When people are encouraged to give, and they give bountifully, they will definitely receive bountifully and , and they will enjoy a pressed down , shaken together and running over blessing.

"But this I say: He who sows sparingly will also reap sparingly, and he who sows bountifully will also reap bountifully."
   II Corinthians 9:6 NKJV

This book is a testimonial book on my experiences and other peoples' experiences on the Miracles of Working Talents. Working Talents changed my life and it has changed lives of many others. In our church when they announce that its a year of working Talents , almost everyone will join in, because people have seen by experience that there is always a positive financial shift to those who obey and work to bring money in the house of the Lord.

"If you are willing and obedient, You shall eat the good of the land;"
  Isaiah 1:19 NKJV

1. My Background

No one would understand why Talents has become such an important topic in my life, unless I share where God has taken me from. When I talk about poverty, I really know what it is all about, because I have experienced poverty in my upbringing and I have lived it. That animal called poverty is not a joke or theory but its reality and it's a demon that can only be dealt with through giving to God, giving to God and to his work, helping the poor and good works in general. In this book I concentrate on Talents, where every person is given an opportunity to become financially useful to the Kingdom of God and work hard to pour money to the work of God and in turn the Lord releases a blessing in their lives.

When I talk about a blessing, some people automatically think about money. Money is part of it but it's not everything. A blessing includes, peace , joy, good health, protection, children who are blessed with good marriages, grand children who carry a blessing in their blood stream, and a good life. It includes blessed hands that causes all you touch to prosper, good sleep when it's time to sleep, and a good appetite when it's time to eat. Some people have a good expensive bed, but they do not enjoy a good sleep. A good sleep does not come cheaply to them, they have to take sleeping tablets just to sleep. Some have fridges full of food, but they have no appetite, they have to take some tablets to have just a good appetite. You might not have thousands of dollars in your bank account but when you have all the above you are blessed, and whenever a need arises, the need is met, you do not live a life of lack, you are very blessed.

In my church Forward In Faith Church, we have thousands of building in more than 146 nations, thousands of cars all over the world, National Centers all over the world including UK, Australia, New Zealand ,to name a few and all this acquired for CASH, no credit, no mortgage. The church owns houses that are bought on cash, and we do not even fuel our cars on credit or using a credit card. That is what I call a blessing and living in the Kingdom, the blessing of the Lord that makes rich and adds no sorrow with it.

"The blessing of the Lord makes one rich, And He adds no sorrow with it."
Proverbs 10:22 NKJV

BORN POOR

I was born in a rural area of Zimbabwe, in Msana TTL. Mugabe village, which is 40km out of Harare the Capital City of Zimbabwe. I am the 7th born in a family of eight., four girls and four boys and I am the fourth girl.
I grew up in a very poor family. If you are born poor, grow up poor, the problem is you will not even know you are poor, that kind of life is your normal, you do not know anything better. We used to walk about eight kilometres to go to school, bare foot. In

the winter we would have neither sweater (jersey) nor shoes. By the time we got to school we would be freezing. The classrooms have no heating. That was life and it was our normal. We got acclimatized.

Toilets were for those who were better than us, they had blair toilets. We used the bush toilet for the longest time. Toilet paper was the leaves from the bushes around. We actually knew which leaves were good and which ones would not cause itching. There was no bathroom at the house, we all bathed in the river. Clothes were old and torn. We rarely got new clothes. My parents could not afford that luxury. At one time my clothes were so torn that part of my body was exposed. I would wear that one dress both for school and at home. On Saturday I would go with my mother to the river, she would wash the dress, sometimes with no soap, and spread it on a tree or stone to dry. I would wait until its almost dry, then I just put it on like that. I cannot remember ever having an underwear. It was a luxury, I only had one later in life.

Food was sadza (our staple food, thick porridge made from corn meal) and pumpkin leaves, or rape leaves or okra. Meat was a very rare commodity. Breakfast was that cornmeal porridge sometimes with no sugar.

Sometimes we would eat sadza with roasted nuts, or pumpkin seeds. Sometimes there would be no relish and my mother would just cook sadza and she puts some salt or sugar in a plate, pour some water and stir and we just dip the sadza in the salty or sugary solution and eat.

When going to school, lunch pack would be roasted corn wrapped in a khaki paper or if its season for mangoes, you just pick some 2 mangoes from under the mango tree and you are good to go.

The girls (my sisters and I) had a hut that was our bedroom. We slept on the floor and shared two blankets, one on the floor and another one to cover all 4 of us. I would always sleep in the middle. It was the culture that the older ones would sleep on the outer side of the blanket and the younger ones in between. I usually made my sisters life very miserable because I would sometimes wet the blankets while I was sleeping in the middle. They would complain, shout or even pinch me but it did not help, because there were no spare blankets and nothing to do except just sleep in the wet blankets. My mother on the other hand was very loving and protective, when it was very cold, she would bring a sack and just throw it on top of us so that we could be warm. Actually, when I was still very young and was still sleeping in their bedroom, I had no blanket, she would just cover me with my father's torn jacket.

Like I said before, I never knew that we were poor. That was the only life I knew, and I thought it was the normal life.

Later my father started to go to church, I do not know whether he got saved, but at least he was now going with my mother to our local Salvation Army church. Things changed a little and my father got a job in Harare, at Ratanje shoe Repairs and that was quite a milestone in our family. That gave me an opportunity to go to High School. None of my sisters had gone for High School, I was the first girl to go to High School. By God's grace my father got a Council house to rent and I and my brothers (my sisters were all married by then)went to live in Harare and I attended High School at Mabvuku Secondary School. Life was a little bit better, I now had a pair of shoes and school uniform. My bedroom was the kitchen, that's where I slept on the floor. My father actually put a lodger in one of the 4 rooms , can you imagine

1. MY BACKGROUND

that? I guess he could not afford rent, so he used one bedroom, my brothers the other bedroom and I slept in the kitchen.

I finished high School and got a job. Both my brother, the one I come after, and I were now working but the truth is you cannot deal with the spirit of poverty overnight. It will follow you and sometimes you do not even know you are poor, especially when life becomes a little better from what you know.

I had never seen or used a toilet with a seat until the time I was in High School. I visited my English female teacher at her home in the Avenues in Zimbabwe, (She liked me because I was very good at English, my essays were usually displayed on the notice boards, I believe God was preparing me to be an Author.) When I went to her home, I asked to use the toilet and I was shown the toilet, I had never seen such a toilet before. At home and at school they had the hole kind of toilet. I struggled in there not knowing how to use the toilet. Finally, I climbed on top, stepping on the seat. You can guess what happened. I messed the floor. What an embarrassment.

Today I see the grace of God, looking back where the Lord took me from and where I am now. I say grace because some people I went to school with are still right there in the same village, they got married in the same village and their children are still going to the same school we went to, still walking those 8 kilometers bare foot. Some of my friends I went to High School with never made it out of Mabvuku. They had their children there, they never drove a car, their families are just going around the same circle.

With this background, I do not play when it comes to giving to God. I work for God for two reasons;

1) To make sure we become a blessed generation, that my offspring will never ever go through what I went through.

2) Secondly to thank God for saving me, for delivering me out of poverty, for bringing me to a church that taught me and encouraged me to give to God .

My life has completely changed, I am blessed. My children are blessed. I am rich and no longer poor. It's all by the grace of God and as I began to work for God, He took me from one glory to the other and he is still shifting me , making my life a living testimony to those who knew me before.

Working Talents has specifically changed my life. Just the word Talents, brings excitement to me. There has always been big breakthroughs after working Talents. New windows of blessings are opened. New windows of opportunity manifest after working Talents.

Talents Oh Yeah!!!

2. A Training School

My first understanding of Talents was that it is a Training School, to train me to make money using my hands, my skill or my profession. Talents will train me to pray so that God can reveal to me avenues to make money, first for God then for myself.

The first time I heard about Talents, I had been in the church for 2 years. I was in a place called Zvishavane and I was not working. We had moved to Zvishavane because my husband who worked as an Electrician had been offered a job by Shabani Mine. That was in 1988.

It was a time in life when I thought selling stuff was embarrassing. I did not know that selling stuff is called a "small business."

Selling vegetables, selling tomatoes, selling fruits for a little profit are the first stages of getting into business and having a business mind.

That year I was taught to knit jerseys (sweaters) for children. My pastor taught me to knit. I had never knitted before. The moment you decide to work for God, God blesses the work of your hands. I would finish a jersey in a day and I got a lot of orders because the jerseys were so beautiful. I made money for the Lord but not only that; after church Talents I knitted jerseys for sale and I also knitted for my family.

I also leant to always be selling some things so as to get some extra money for the family and for myself.

Talents is a training school that teaches one to be disciplined in money matters. If I have my Talents money in the bag and I am walking in the mall, I am very disciplined not start shopping using that money. I know it's not my money, it's God's money and I have to keep it until I take it to church.

Most of all I discovered that working Talents is a training school to give God in a big way, provoking God and thereby unlocking my miracles through working Talents. Big things in my life and my husband's life have happened only after working Talents. There has been big breakthroughs, big blessings and big financial shifts. Big projects that needed large sums of money became easy after working Talents.

Therefore, Talents is a training school to make money and also to be able to give God big amounts of money that I am not able to give all other times. It is an opportunity to change my measure in the area of giving. It is only through Talents that my husband and I have been able to give God big amounts like ten thousand, twelve thousand, seventeen thousand, twenty thousand , twenty-one thousand, twenty-five thousand, even thirty thousand. God has made it possible to work these amounts in a time space of 10 months (Talents are worked January to October.) By the way we do not work Talents every year but once in three to five years. After the church Talents , the year following will be Home Talents. This is when we say God will be saying, "Continue with what you were doing, and I will bless the works of your hands."

Then the king said to Araunah, "No, but I will surely buy it from you for a price; nor will I offer burnt offerings to the

Lord my God with that which costs me nothing." So, David bought the threshing floor and the oxen for fifty shekels of silver.
  II Samuel 24:24 NKJV

In Talents we learn to give God an offering that costs us something. Not change or money that I do not need, but I give myself to God first and say I am available to be a vessel to bring money into your house first and then do my own things later.

"And not only as we had hoped, but they first gave themselves to the Lord, and then to us by the will of God."
  II Corinthians 8:5

In Talents we give ourselves first then allow God to use us to raise money to build churches or do big projects that need big sums of money. We only have one life and it will soon be past but only what is done for Christ will last. Talents is an opportunity to have a record on earth and in heaven, a good record of affecting the Kingdom financially, to be financially useful in the Kingdom of God.

Those who understand Talents, will stop all personal projects in the year of working Talents in order to concentrate on the projects of God, then do our projects the year we do the home Talents, and we always see God doing great things in our lives.

"Thus, speaks the Lord of hosts, saying: 'This people says, "The time has not come, the time that the Lord 's house should be built." ' " Then the word of the Lord came by

Haggai the prophet, saying, " Is it time for you yourselves to dwell in your paneled houses, and this temple to lie in ruins?"
Haggai 1:2-4 NKJV

So, the year of Talents is not a year to compete with the Lord and do your own thing, but it's a time to serve God with my finances. Surely my own project can wait until I finish the Lord's projects.

It's a training to put God first, a training to run with the things of God first then do mine later, a training to put importance in the things of God, and training to share my resources with God.

It is a training to get out of debt, a training to make extra money for myself and the family so that I do not just rely on a salary. Salary is not enough and will never be enough no matter how much you earn, but Talents is the key to do business and be an entrepreneur.

It's a training school to be able to save and to be disciplined when it comes to money. I do not use the money for Talents for my personal use, but I put it aside and take it to church and the discipline will continue even after Talents. Talents have taught me to go into a shop with a lot of money in my bag and not use it because I have been taught to discipline myself. As long as it's not for shopping it will not be used for shopping.

One year I just decided to seriously work Talents for one reason, to be Favored by God (kufarirwa naMwari) and from that year I have experienced grace after grace and favour after favour. It was my opportunity to catch the attention of God. I was still an elder then, and that year my husband and I worked Seventeen Thousand Dollars. , I cannot remember all the other amounts I worked prior to that, but this amount I will not forget because

2. A TRAINING SCHOOL

that was my turning point and the year my husband and I decided to work talents outstandingly. We changed our measure in giving God and God changed His measure of blessing us .

Working Talents is your opportunity to fly high in the things of God, to excel in God and in life. to tap into another level of blessings and another level of miraculous gathering of money. As you hold God's money there is definitely going to be a financial residue that is left in your life.

Talents are not for the heathens, Talents are for children of God. It's an inhouse thing, creating a reason for God to bless you.

Talents Oh Yeah - the best way to unlock my miracles!!

3. A Willing Heart

"**S**peak to the children of Israel, that they bring Me an offering. From everyone who gives it willingly with his heart you shall take My offering."
Exodus 25:2 NKJV

The number one qualification to work Talents is , a willing heart. In working Talents God is not looking for those with money, or big businesses but he is looking for those with a willing heart. God already has the money, but he is looking for people that he can use as channels to bring his money into his church. A willing heart is the way to invite God to use you as his channel.

The moment a person hears about Talents and their heart is not excited, they see it as a burden. They think the church wants to take their money, they have denied themselves the opportunity to allow God to use them as a channel.

Many times, I have met people with an attitude of , Wow my money, the church wants to take my money and I usually ask in preaching, WHICH MONEY?

because most of these people do not even have five thousand dollars in their bank account , not even two thousand or one thousand. When they hear about Talents their first thought is , my money, which money?

God actually want to use people like you and me who have

3. A WILLING HEART

nothing so that when we are able to give Ten thousand to God in ten months, or twenty thousand or fifty thousand then we know very well it was God but not us. Who can raise such an amount in a short time unless its God using them. Like I said the moment you become a channel for God to bless his church, there is definitely going to be some financial residue in your life and God will use the same method you used, for you to raise that money, to bless you after the church Talents.

Do not protect money that you do not have in the first place. God is not after your money, he just want a willing heart. He uses those with a willing heart to transfer wealth into his kingdom.

One year I was pastoring a church in Ruwa Zimbabwe. We had someone come to our women's meeting and encourage us on Talents. She really stirred us up, so much that when we left the meeting to me nothing else mattered except working Talents. There was real fire in my Spirit. I felt like this woman was a Noah calling to say "come let's build the Ark."

Many people ignored the call, they were busy with their own things, they were busy with their projects, they thought this old man was crazy, where is the flood, there is no sign of rain. They did not want to be bothered, they had more important things to do. Unfortunately, they never stayed in those beautiful houses they were building, they never made the money they so badly wanted to make. They were swept away by the flood. If only they had listened to Noah with spiritual ears. It is the same with Talents, all God's things must be heard with spiritual ears. God never forces anyone. He just wants a willing heart.

That year in Ruwa after being stirred up by the preacher, I went home and could not sleep. I left my husband in bed and sneaked out of the bed into the lounge to pray. I was crying and asking

God to give me money, to open doors for me to make money for the Lord. I felt fire in my Spirit. I wanted to be one of the women in my church who is outstanding when it comes to giving to the work of God. I was tired of the Spirit of being AVERAGE, I wanted to excel. I wanted my name written in heaven and on earth as a woman who affects the Kingdom financially. I wanted to play my number and leave a mark in my generation. (kuita chikadzi chinozivikanwa nekushandira Mwari).

I was tired of being ordinary, tired of the same old testimony, tired of being in the big group of Other Women. I cried that night. Crying and praying because my heart was extremely willing. Everything else did not matter at that moment because all that was in me wanted to do something outstanding for my God.

At 3am my land line phone rang, and I was surprised. Who could be calling at such a time. It was my associate pastor, Kudzie Kahwema. I said to her, "Is everything ok?" In my Shona language I would say, "kwakanaka here?" She answered crying, " No , nothing is ok here, I am sick because of Talents" (ndarwara neTarenda ini). We both started crying, and I told her, "Me too I am in prayer, I am awake, I cannot sleep."

When one is stirred up in that manner and to that extent, you know God has chosen you as a vessel . A willing heart leads to prayer and prayer will bring ideas of how to get the money , prayer will bring about a figure, a target in your spirit and you start praying towards your target.

If you hear about Talents and you are not bothered, you do not care whether you will work or not, you do not even have a desire to raise a certain amount of money, you look at Talents as a burden or a bother, it shows you have not found grace, God is refusing your contribution to his work. Others are having

3. A WILLING HEART

sleepless nights but you! day after day you sleep soundly. You are missing your blessings somewhere.

As I am writing this book, December 2018, I am in the USA and a leader of the women in our church in that nation. From the time Talents were announced by our mother Apostle Eunor when she came to the USA in June 2018, I have had no rest. The burden to do something outstanding kept on growing bigger and bigger. I started praying on my own but as the burden grew bigger, I felt like inviting every woman in the USA to a time of fasting and prayer. We have just finished 21 days of fasting and praying, we were meeting on the teleconference line to pray 5 days a week, Monday to Friday. For me and a few others it was 21 days of having soup, a cup of tea and water only. A desperate situation needs a desperate measure.

We are tired of our nation being the tail when it comes to working for God, we are coming from a long way, but we will get there. Some men said we also want to join the fast for 2019 Talents and they joined.

The people are on fire, people are confessing big figures. We are believing God for a bumper harvest in 2019. I looked back and thought, have I ever fasted for talents before we get into the year of Talents and I saw that never before, that alone shows me that God is up to something great in 2019. What the eye has not seen, nor the ear heard!!

Watch out Zimbabwe, watch out South Africa your rand will not stand, watch out UK and Australia, America is on fire!!!! And we will be the pace setters in the 2019 Talents, we are already ahead in prayer and fasting because our hearts have been stirred up and we are more than willing to go at once and possess our National

Centre for Jesus!!

"And let us consider one another in order to stir up love and good works,"
   Hebrews 10:24

The burden to write this book came during this fast, I felt like I could not keep what is boiling in my heart to myself, I need to impart this to some women who are tired of being ordinary. I shared with my parents Apostles Ezekiel and Eunor Guti and they blessed me, Prof Ezekiel actually recorded a foreword for me!!

Fellow pastors, elders and deacons, we are well able to do it, with God nothing shall be impossible.

2019 Talents , I am going to work like an Overseer, like a big respected woman in our church (semukadzi mukuru). The young women in my church must have somewhere to look up to.

"For we dare not class ourselves or compare ourselves with those who commend themselves. But they, measuring themselves by themselves, and comparing themselves among themselves, are not wise."
   II Corinthians 10:12 NKJV

In Talents do not compare yourselves with yourself, hear what others are doing. Send teams to other people's big Days, be motivated and provoked by others.

I am a woman who believes in being number one, number one for the church I lead, number one for the region I lead, number one for the province or nation I lead. Why settle for

3. A WILLING HEART

mediocrity when excellence is there? Number two is not part of my vocabulary. Talents oh Yeah!!! I am not going to position myself with believers and deacons, but I will take my rightful position as someone who has been entrusted with much!!

Talents oh Yeah, deacons it's your time to prove who you are in the Lord. Elders this is the time to be outstanding. In our church, you can be a prayer warrior, a praise and worshipper and many others, but if we fail to find you when it comes to working for our God, contributing to buying buildings and houses of worship for our God, we start thinking you do not really belong with us, we begin to doubt if you are genuine. The church is looking for elders and deacons who stand with the church financially. Elders and deacons who are financially useful to the Kingdom of God. 2019 is your year to make a difference.

Talents Oh Yeah!!!

4. Confession of Faith!

"You will also declare a thing, And it will be established for you; So, light will shine on your ways."
Job 22:28 NKJV

As one becomes extremely excited about Talents or working Talents, figures of money will start to be dropped in your spirit. It might start small but the more you are stirred up , the figure will go up. Do not be afraid or intimidated to confess the figure that the Lord put on your heart. It's now the Holy Spirit working in you, dropping in your spirit a figure that you never imagined possible. It's not your number, it's the Holy Spirit speaking through you, that same Holy Spirit will make it possible for you to work that figure. Its spiritual. Do not limit the Holy Spirit. Also, it's not a pledge, it's a target. A target means I would have wanted to work that figure by God's grace. A target is a desire, and no one will arrest you for desiring. When the desire is there, " Confess it!!". You shall declare a thing and it shall be established to you. Say it out!! Talk about it (Bvotomoka) others say it's ' hallucinating' things that seem impossible in the physical, but they are truly there in the Spirit. People who hallucinate in real life will be seeing things that we cannot see in the physical. So, we confess things by faith.

4. CONFESSION OF FAITH!

"Now faith is the substance of things hoped for, the evidence of things not seen."
Hebrews 11:1 NKJV

Let me give you a testimony of what happened in 2001. It was a year of Talents. It was my first year as a pastor, we had just finished Bible School in 2000 had been deployed to Ruwa as associate pastors.

As we were going to our Women's Tuesday Prayers in Harare Zimbabwe, we were confessing figures and that time with inflation, we were going into millions, but that time a million was still a lot of money. For you to understand the value of it, a million that time could buy 4 or 5 houses in the low-density areas. Houses in very good areas that time were going for $200 000 to $300 000. Those who had held a million were the real rich people.

Our mother Apostle Eunor Guti , one day, at the beginning of Talents came to the Tuesday prayer and confessed that she felt that some people will work a Million dollars plus on these Talents. She then said the number that the Holy Spirit had impressed on her heart was 2 million and above. That was what she wanted to work, that was her number, her target. Oh my God!!! that was a shocking figure. Everyone was surprised and could not process this information. She prophetically said some women would work one million, some half a million and so on. But she said the secret was to confess it and believe God was going to do it.

Oh !!! this topic became very controversial. Remember we were women only and when the men heard it, some said, "Mai Guti is now going astray with all the women". How can she talk about such figures? If other people from other churches hear this, they will think we are crazy.

Some men would say, "You women , do you know how many zeros a million has, do you even know how to write a million? Why do you confess things that are impossible???"

Even some women joined the mentality of the men and refused to confess or talk about a million because they said it was crazy.

The following week Mama Guti came wearing a T. Shirt that was written " Mrs 2 Million plus." She was not going back on her confession. Whether or not she knew what people were saying I do not know. I heard some men were planning to tell our father, Apostle E. H. Guti (her husband) to say please put some sense in her.

When Apostle Eunor came wearing her "Mrs 2 million plus" T-shirt she was also selling some T. Shirts that were written Mrs 1 million plus . She said those who believed with her for big monies can buy the T. Shirts and wear their confession. I was very stirred, and I liked Mama Guti' s boldness to talk about Millions.

We used to sing , " I am a millionaire, I am a millionaire! Millionaire!!"

We would go on to sing leaning on another millionaire (zembera millionaire) and I decided I also want to lean on our mother who was confessing millions.

I also bought my T-shirt which was written " Mrs 1 million plus" and I was geared up and began to confess a million plus. Those days you really needed to know who to talk to and who to listen to. Even some of the leaders in the church would discourage us to speak about millions, as a young pastor I never really argued with anyone, but I would continue to confess about a million and I continued to wear my t-shirt. Sometimes I would be mocked

4. CONFESSION OF FAITH!

about it by fellow pastors.

When working Talents, know who to talk to and know who to befriend. Do not befriend people who are always negative, people who critisise the vision. In our church we have been working Talents for more than 50 years, and people's lives have been changed. People have been delivered from poverty. I myself have been in this church for more than 32 years, the more years the more excitement for Talents. Seriously, there must be something good I have experienced and seen through working Talents. Refuse to be discouraged. Some people are used by the devil to discourage others thereby depriving them of their blessings.

When your target is big, you start thinking big. If your target is small, you think small.

That year I began to think big. I was selling roasted nuts, in a small dish, but I began to see that I will not raise enough with the small dish. There was a tuck-shop, (convenience shop or daily shop) right opposite our house. My clientele had only been our church people, but I started thinking of taking my nuts business outside church. I approached the owner of that tuck-shop and asked him whether I could bring my nuts and they can help me sell them. He used to respect us a lot because most of our church members who visited our house bought from his shop. This man had more than ten big tuck-shops in that suburb. His business dominated in that area.

He said, " No problem Pastor, you can bring your nuts. Prepare a lot of nuts and bring some here, then find more containers and place a big dish at each of my stores. Take the nuts to all my shops, in the morning and in the evening come collect your money. I do not want my girls to mix your money with my money, so they will put yours aside, just make sure every evening you go round collecting your money and, in the morning, bring more packets of nuts." Isn't God amazing. I was excited.

Now my problem was to meet the demand. I spent sleepless nights roasting the nuts in a small pan and my maid and family helping me to pack.

One day my brother visited me. He is a well up person. He was not coming to our church then, but now he is a deacon. He saw all the trouble. He was moved to support me. He said there had to be a way to roast more nuts at one time.

The following day, he brought me a nut roasting machine. It was an improvised thing, a drum cut on one side with a lid, where you could pour 50kgs of nuts. It had some gas fire at the bottom and you only had to turn the handle and roast 50kgs of peanuts at one time.

If you are willing ,God will make a way. Now my job was just to pack the nuts and deliver. God made a way. That business continued until I left Ruwa 5 years later.

That year as I continued to think Big, I acted big. We hired a 5 tonne truck and went to Chipinge in Zimbabwe to order pineapples. No more pineapples in a dish but in a lorry, 5 tonne truck. We faced some challenges here and there, but we still made some profit.

A certain deacon, the one I call Mujuda in my other book (change your measure) saw that I was thinking big and she came with an idea. She had heard there was a great shortage of potatoes in Zambia and she heard people were making a lot of money. She said, " Let's get a 5 tonne truck and order bags of potatoes and take them to Zambia to sell." I was for it.

We went to Zambia, faced a lot of problems at the border, because we had not made enough research. We spent five days

4. CONFESSION OF FAITH!

at the border and finally we were allowed to pass. Some of the potatoes were rotten because of that long stay on the border. We still went. When you work for God, it does not mean you will not face challenges or problems. The way to learn more on a certain business is through challenges. Challenges bring experience.

We had to repack some bags and throw away the rotten potatoes, but praise be to God, I brought home $40 000 for talents out of that trip. That deacon (she was a deacon then) and her husband, said the Lord had spoken to them to give me all the profits made of that trip.

When working Talents, the devil will try to discourage us in many different ways, but God will see us through. God respects every effort.

I was still confessing my 1 million plus.

One day I was at the Tuesday prayer, a certain pastor came to me and asked to talk to me outside. We went outside, this pastor said something very funny, but she encouraged me. I liked her attitude and I love challenges. Her name is Priscilla Gono, and she was pastoring in Chitungwiza then, Zengeza 4. She said to me , " Young woman , I have been watching you, I see a lot of potential in you, I have also heard good things about the work you are doing in Ruwa. I called you here to challenge you. What do you think about some of these Districts that are being wasted, where the female DPs are unproductive? Let's work hard and take over those districts, don't you want to drive a church car too as you come for Tuesday prayer? The only way for that to happen is to work outstandingly, be made district pastors next year and we will drive those cars. Let's do it for God and God will do it for us."

She said that was all she had called me for and from that day we became friends who just encouraged each other and shared ideas.

To cut a long story short, at the end of those Talents, Apostle Eunor worked the 2 Million she was confessing. Amongst the Pastors I remember 2 worked 1 million plus, I the young disciple worked $200 000. I was running towards my million. $200 000 at that time could buy a house in the low-density areas. It was a lot of money. Amongst the pastors in our province Harare East my husband and I were on number 5. It was very impressive because it was our first year as pastors.

Working Talents will open doors of opportunity for you. That year, not the following year, but end of that year we were promoted. Our senior had worked $30 000 and the young pastors who agreed to confess big worked $170 000 more. I strongly suspect the working hard brought about the promotion. Just one year after Bible School we were given the District, we moved to Windsor Park into a big and better house where the DP used to stay.

That friend of mine Priscilla also worked $200 000 and was also promoted. The following year we were both driving District cars as we went for the Tuesday prayers.

Talents Oh yeah. That year as a young pastor in the church, I learnt that you do not play with Talents in this church. We are a self-propagating church and we respect pastors who are productive. If you want to be a successful pastor, your name must be among those who are productive, because at the end of the day we want to build churches and buy cars for the work, that alone needs money.

Do not hang around people who speak negatively about your church or who criticize the vision for our church. Those people never go far, they do not succeed. Choose good friends who

4. CONFESSION OF FAITH!

encourage you.

5. Spirit of Joy As We Work Talents

The trend and culture of working Talents is that we give joyfully. We are excited, and we sing joyfully as we give to God. Every time we work Talents, we raise amazing amounts of money and I would like to believe God is provoked with the joy and excitement.

There is something I have noticed. Because our church has grown so big, we have many churches all over the world. The church is in more than 146 Nations and States.

Where ever the people follow the true vision of Talents, and every Sunday leave time to Talents and they sing joyfully as they give to the Lord, that church works outstandingly. But those who are embarrassed to talk about Talents and the leaders do everything hush , hush. Talents monies are not announced, they also do very badly in Talents.

In our church, we do not announce your tithe or offering but we announce your Talents figure because its Public funds, unless you want to be announced as anonymous, we can do that. Talents are usually worked for projects that we are doing as a church, and there must be transparency on who has given what and how much we have raised as an assembly, how much we have raised as a Region or Province, how much we have raised as a Nation, there must be transparency. It also creates and encourages good

5. SPIRIT OF JOY AS WE WORK TALENTS

competition.

Where ever this transparency is compromised, they never raise a lot of money. I thought it was just our church, but I was encouraged to see on TBN , in America, they will have a whole month of raising money for the TV station and people will be calling with their amounts they intend to give, and they will be announcing every amount given. At the end of the month they also announce the total raised. This is the law of Public funds.

In our church there is no one who ever backslid because we are working Talents. What we need to do is to teach the people and cause them to be blessed. We must teach using scriptures, it's the word of God that convinces people. Invite those who are anointed in that area and let them teach your people, otherwise you deprive the people of their blessing.

We learn it from David in the word of God. He led by example, giving towards the building of the temple. He announced publicly how much he was giving and the rest of the leaders of Israel followed suit.

"Moreover, because I have set my affection on the house of my God, I have given to the house of my God, over and above all that I have prepared for the holy house, my own special treasure of gold and silver: three thousand talents of gold, of the gold of Ophir, and seven thousand talents of refined silver, to overlay the walls of the houses; the gold for things of gold and the silver for things of silver, and for all kinds of work to be done by the hands of craftsmen. Who then is willing to consecrate himself this day to the Lord ?"
I Chronicles 29:3-5 NKJV

I was also encouraged recently when I was in Israel. We went to Capernaum - THE TOWN OF OUR LORD JESUS CHRIST. Our tour guide told us about the rich people in Capernaum who greatly supported the ministry of Jesus Christ. Right there in Capernaum there was a temple that was built by these rich people and you could see from the ruins that it used to be a very expensive building. What caught my attention was that on one of the pillars there was a list of names of people who had contributed to the building of this expensive looking building. Even in the times of Jesus they were writing names of those who worked outstandingly, and they even inscribed their names on the wall of the building.

If I was living in Israel during the time of Jesus I would probably be living in Capernaum and my name would be inscribed on that wall. Nevertheless, my name can still be written in heaven and on earth as I support the work of God through working Talents.

In 2015 our father Apostle E. H Guti planted a church in Boston. My husband and I were assigned to nurture the baby church. A few months after he was gone, 2016 was declared to be a year of working Talents. I really struggled on what was the best thing to do. Should I introduce the Talents to these new believers or should I wait?

There was a Women's Conference in California and some speakers spoke on Talents. It was home talents then, but they also explained that the following year was going to be a year of church Talents.

One of the ladies, who is now a pastor in our church, Gertrude Mageza, summoned me to go outside because she wanted to talk to me. Outside, she challenged me and asked me, "Why are you not telling us about Talents, why are you hiding Talents from us?"

5. SPIRIT OF JOY AS WE WORK TALENTS

I was really embarrassed. Another one again, Tanaka Shonhiwa challenged me. Getrude so understood Talents that she said to me, here is my opportunity to get out of debt. I have included Getrude and Tanaka' testimonies among the testimonies in chapter 10.

When I finally, though briefly talked on Talents at our church, everyone grabbed it with excitement. Whenever I would just start a song on Talents everyone would jump up, get their bag, their purse, their bank card and begin to dance and rejoice.

I taught them to never remain seated while others are singing and dancing. If you hold your bag, bank card or purse as a point of contact, God will see the willingness and pour the money. They caught it.

Amazingly, that new church was number one in 2016 Zegu Talents in all the USA Forward in faith churches. The church that followed behind us needed about$ 40 000 to catch up. One of the newly appointed elders then, Violet Gonzo was number one in the whole nation, she worked $60 000. I really believe that the Spirit of joy contributed to the success. Until now they still lead in many areas of Giving. They have a different pastor now, but the Spirit of joy still prevails as they give.

Sadness, grumpiness, angry faces chase away money. Joy brings more money, even in business, in our marriages and in life. Let's be joyous as we work Talents.

This time in the USA we have declared that we sing Talents songs in English, in Nyanja, in Spanish, in Shona, in Ndebele as long as they bring joy and as long as we explain what the song says to the few who cannot understand. As long as the church has one spirit there is no problem with that.

In Boston we had Karen, a white American lady and our now

pastor Ricky also a white American, but we would sing together in English and when we switch to Shona they would sing along. It's all spiritual, we had one spirit and we were successful in working Talents.

Sometimes at the end of the singing and dancing I would pray and call money, and money came.

A lot of those people started new businesses that year through Talents. Travel Agency, home care, Realtors (Estate Agency-selling houses) House flipping to name a few.

Sing joyfully and God will pour some money, make Talents a secret and nothing will happen at your church. You will be at the end of the line.

Some elders or pastors quench the spirit of joy when we are working Talents. As soon as someone stands to talk about giving or talk about money, they are not happy, they interrupt and start saying , "Time up, time up" only when people talk on giving. At all other times they are not bothered about time, only when people want to encourage on Talents that's when they start putting pressure about time.

Some of these people have a spirit of poverty themselves and will cause the whole church they lead to be poor. The concept of giving is very simple, the more the people give, the more they get blessed, the less they give, the poorer they get, and money becomes scarce and scarce.

Let's look at the example of Solomon.
"Now the king went to Gibeon to sacrifice there, for that was the great high place: Solomon offered a thousand burnt offerings on that altar."
I Kings 3:4 NKJV

5. SPIRIT OF JOY AS WE WORK TALENTS

Solomon was a big giver and during his time he caused people to give and the result was, during Solomon's time, silver and gold was like common stones in Jerusalem.

"And these governors, each man in his month, provided food for King Solomon and for all who came to King Solomon's table. There was no lack in their supply. They also brought barley and straw to the proper place, for the horses and steeds, each man according to his charge."
   I Kings 4:27-28 NKJV

Above verses shows a culture of giving during Solomon's time. When there is a culture of giving at a church, there will be no lack. If there is a culture of stinginess at a church, people become financially dry (mari inopwa, inopera).

"All King Solomon's drinking vessels were gold, and all the vessels of the House of the Forest of Lebanon were pure gold. Not one was silver, for this was accounted as nothing in the days of Solomon."
   I Kings 10:21 NKJV

"The king made silver as common in Jerusalem as stones, and he made cedar trees as abundant as the sycamores which are in the lowland."
   I Kings 10:27

I was talking to one of the elders from one of the places we once pastored (me and my husband). When I was there, money was very plenteous in the church and in people's lives. Many thought it was just happening on its own, new businesses were opened. Raising money was not a problem. At one time we took a love offering of $9 000 in just a few minutes for a speaker who had visited our church. Individuals giving a thousand, two thousand, five thousand , even ten thousand in a service was not a problem. When speakers came to our church they were showered with clothes , money etc. Even among ourselves there was a spirit of giving. It was a giving church. But transfer came and slowly they stopped giving, some even criticizing what we used to do. Money was still there and to them it was just happening on its own.

But also, slowly, the money began to get lesser and lesser in their lives because they stopped giving as a church. Of course, a few individuals continued, and they were still being blessed. At one time I visited the same place and was shocked that the same church was struggling to raise a little amount of money, same church that used to give so big. Money had dried up because they stopped giving.

The elder said, "If you see us raising small amounts of money for projects or struggling to raise money, do not think that we are stingy, no we are not stingy, but money is no longer there, it has dried up."

That is very true when it comes to giving, when you stop giving then money disappears, doors of money close up. You give , and encourage the church to give, money becomes plenty.

It also happened when we were pastoring in Christchurch New Zealand. We worked Talents very outstandingly and there was abundance of finances in people's lives. Money was everywhere. The New Zealand dollar became cheap. People were blessed even as they worked Talents. That year our church raised $450 000 in ten months. For a small church of about 120 people that was awesome.

When it came to just general giving, a person giving a thousand dollars or more in one service was very common. When we were

5. SPIRIT OF JOY AS WE WORK TALENTS

giving, I would call out, "Those with a thousand or more please come give your offering" and a number of people 5, 6 or seven would boldly walk up and give a thousand dollars and more, and I would call out again and say: " those with $500 or more come up" and another group would come up, those kind of figures were so common. I would go down to $300 and son on and end at $50 and below. Silver and gold was like common stones.

Sometimes I would start on a thousand and some elders like Jeff Gohwa would shout, "Pastor you are Limiting us," and I would say go to $2000 and he would still shout " You are still limiting us." Elders Jeff, Denford Mukundu and Irvin Kombora would challenge each other unto good works.

When we finished Talents and we were getting into home Talents, I do not know what entered into them. In a meeting they said, "This year we have been working for God, next year its a year of Home Talents. We will be raising money for us and our families, please no church projects. Leave us free to work for ourselves."

We agreed with them. After all they had worked very hard that year. But something happened, as they stopped giving to the work of God, money did not come as easy as it did when they were sharing with God. Six months down the line, they realised that when they stopped giving to the work of God, money dwindled. They discussed among themselves and called us and said, "We made a very big mistake, we did not realise that a lot of money was coming our way because we were giving to God but when we stopped giving God and concentrated on ourselves, money began to dry up. Let's do some church projects immediately." ha ha ha!!

We thank God for an opportunity to work Talents as a church, it's an opportunity to be blessed as a church.

The year of Talents, my husband and I will do some projects that God allows us to do to raise money and we also just say, "Whatever money God blesses us with (outside our allowance) we share half to half with God." We have since realised that it's in the year of Talents that we end up having whatever comes to us, what we remain with, is much better than all the other years that we are not working Talents.

The year of Talents is a year of all-round abundance. It's a year when God releases an abundance of finances which is enjoyed by those who work Talents willingly, not being forced, not being persuaded but with a willing heart.
"But this I say: He who sows sparingly will also reap sparingly, and he who sows bountifully will also reap bountifully. So, let each one give as he purposes in his heart, not grudgingly or of necessity; for God loves a cheerful giver."
    II Corinthians 9:6-7 **NKJV**

Talents Oh yeah

6. Talents Rounds (Money Clubs)

"**Now the multitude of those who believed were of one heart and one soul; neither did anyone say that any of the things he possessed was his own, but they had all things in common."**
Acts 4:32 NKJV

These are some of the strategies we use in working Talent, strategies that help us reach our goal, strategies where we work as a team to achieve great results in gathering money for our God. Team work helps us encourage and motivate each other.

It was in 1994 when I was an Elder in Bulawayo when I first learnt we could do these rounds for Talents. We used to do rounds for other things and sometimes at work with work mates, even at church with fellow church members, these helped us save for furniture, kitchen utensils etc.

A round is when a number of women or men, decide to help each other save for something. It could be just saving money, or they could all have one thing in common that they all want, and they want to help each other and work co-operatively to achieve their goal.

Let's say ten people, they all have a desire to buy a car each, or they want to save $10 000 each in ten months. They get together, make a plan to all contribute $1 000 each and give to one person the first month. That person can buy their car or use the money for what they intended to save for. The next month they do the same again, give the 2nd person ten thousand. They position themselves in the order they agree on. There are others who usually want to be given first, some they always want to be given last. So usually they have a meeting first and discuss the order of receiving the money.

They continue giving one person after another each month, until they all achieve their goal. Of course, every person could have saved the ten thousand on their own, but this round or money club gives each person discipline and commitment to save. Something they might not have achieved by doing it on their own. When you do this on your own, if another need comes up you can change your mind and use the money for another need. When you join a round you cannot change your mind in the middle of it, you have to show integrity to the other members.

This way of saving is very common in the African culture, starting from as little as $5 or $10 a day or a week. It could be 5 women selling some vegetables at a market and they agree to give each other $10 a day for 5 days. So, on Monday all the five contribute $10 each and give to one lady $50 and the next day they give the next one in line and third day they contribute and give the third one and so each week they are able to save $50 from their sales.

In short, it's a way to help each other reach a goal. To me it's a sign of UNITY! It can only be done when brethren dwell together in unity. (Psalms 133)

"Behold, how good and how pleasant it is For brethren to dwell together in unity! It is like the precious oil upon the head, Running down on the beard, The beard of Aaron,

6. TALENTS ROUNDS (MONEY CLUBS)

Running down on the edge of his garments. It is like the dew of Hermon, Descending upon the mountains of Zion; For there the Lord commanded the blessing— Life forevermore."
Psalms 133:1-3 NKJV

Yes, it is a unity thing, you have to be friends or get on well to plan a round or money club together.

I have learnt that there are many cultures who practice this too. One of them are Indians. Most Indians own some business of some sort. They do these rounds, I am told, of big amounts like ten thousand dollars a month or every two months among ten people. One person receives $100 000 and uses it to set up a business. The next receives and uses the money to also set up theirs until they all have set up their businesses.

My first-born daughter, Blessing Diana and Chris her husband , about 3 years ago, got into a round with friends from their Forward In Faith Melbourne church, in Australia. They all wanted to save money to use as deposit towards purchasing a house. They were about six professional couples and were contributing $5 000 each couple and they all achieved their goal. We visited our daughter end of 2017 and they had just moved into a beautiful brand-new house which they had had built. The round money helped them to raise the deposit that was needed, and they achieved their goal. It was part of their home Talents project.

For anyone to qualify into any round, they need to be extremely faithful and trusty worthy. I know some people who cannot join one single round now because they are not faithful. They defaulted in a number of groups and now they have been " black listed" so to speak. They start saying stories and giving excuses after they have been given their share and are not faithful to give back what they have received.

At every church or work place or in the community, there are people who if you mention them, when arranging a group, everyone shouts "No!"

It is not a good sign especially to the children of God. It shows lack of discipline or trustworthiness.

So, in 1994 when I was an Elder in Bulawayo, my Overseer then introduced a round of $1000 per month for Talents. There were ten of us. Oh, that round helped me to achieve my goal. I had a desire to work $20 000 that year. It was my Target. I ended up raising $17 000 in that year of Talents. I had never worked such a big amount before. I managed to raise the amount very easily because $10 000 of it came from the rounds. The other $7 000, is what I contributed above my round money. So, every month I would make sure I have the money for the round first, give it to the one receiving and then continue working so I could also give above the $1000. It worked for me and have done it with fellow church members every time we are working Talents. It speeds up my goal for Talents and helps me achieve it. I did not reach my target but was almost there and the money club helped me to be disciplined and focused on my target.

Usually among the group, there is a chairperson. In the old days all of us would give the money to the Chairperson who would then take the money to the church and have it receipted under the name of the person whose turn it was. You would not even touch the money, in case you changed your mind and diverted from our goal. So, we would help you by handling the money and taking it to church for you. You only got the receipt.

6. TALENTS ROUNDS (MONEY CLUBS)

With technology these days it's even easier. In the US we no longer give the money to any person. We deposit the money straight into an account that we use to receive the funds. When a person deposits their money, they post the deposit slip on our WhatsApp group chat as proof of deposit. We give each other a deadline of when the money should be in the account. We can say from the end of the month to the 5th of the following month. By that time the money should be in the account. It's usually before the monthly Big day date. When all people in the group have deposited their monies, its transferred to the Talents account and the secretary given proof and asked to receipt the amount which is already in the Talents account. No more handling any money.

To me I have found out that these money clubs help me to reach my target or come close to my target. Usually when I join the $1000 round and we are 10, then I already know that I am above the 10 thousand amount. I just discipline myself to make sure the $1000 is there every month and then I work hard to work some more money to give outside the round I will be contributing. If you are a person of integrity, you keep up with your payments because you do not want a bad name, or to disappoint your team members, you aim to be a good team player and it helps you reach your goal.

From 1994 when I started to join a Talents round, I have always used rounds in working Talents and encouraged others to join them. It gives me an opportunity to be able to give a big amount at one time. In Christchurch, in the first year of working Talents there, we were 7 and each month one of us was giving $7 000 for Talents. It really provoked others and the next time we worked Talents many joined, and we had 2 groups of 10 people in the $1000 group and another 2 groups of $500 each with ten people in each group. It meant that every month as a church we had a minimum amount of $30 000 being given towards Talents without fail, from the groups only. We found ourselves being able to raise big amounts like $50 000 ,$65 000 and highest we raised in one month was $76 000. It's a very simple but efficient way to help people work for their God and it helps them change their measure in giving. Luke 6 vs 38.

"Give, and it will be given to you: good measure, pressed down, shaken together, and running over will be put into your bosom. For with the same measure that you use, it will be measured back to you."
Luke 6:38 NKJV

It all comes down to more blessings.
"But this I say: He who sows sparingly will also reap sparingly, and he who sows bountifully will also reap bountifully."
II Corinthians 9:6 NKJV

We also did the same for the home Talents and that year every month we were giving two families $10 000 each in church on our big day and another 2 families $5 000 each. Even some people in the community were moved and liked our church for it, they had never seen such unity and team work in helping each other save money.

Most of the ladies I did rounds with in Christchurch were professional women. They were working talents with many other different projects but the money for the round specifically came from what we used to call (R.R.P.P). RESE RESE PESE PESE. This means working any kind of job, anywhere, as a general worker.

Most of these ladies. Sandy Mkundu, Lilian Kombora, Joyce

6. TALENTS ROUNDS (MONEY CLUBS)

Matavire, Clara Gohwa to mention a few, would go to their regular jobs 9am to 5pm Monday through Friday. But two days a week they would pick RRPP at a nearby local Aged Care Facility and that money was enough for the round. Even when we did the home talents they continued with the same schedules and saved $10 000 in ten months doing RRPP.

In America too, I know ladies like Elder Abigail Mugutso, deacon Julie Chitiyo, who just pick some shifts of RRPP, outside their normal jobs, just for the round. Julie does cleaning and now she has a cleaning business together with Elder Miriam Flores who now owns a cleaning business which came through doing RRPP in Talents. It's a training School.

Find something that gives you consistent income for your round and continue with it after the Talents.

Laws of Successful Rounds (Money Club)

1. **Never force anyone to join a round, if they refuse to participate, they know their capacity, if you force them, they will give you problems.**

2. **Do not put someone in the group that you are not free with or a person you are afraid of, they will give you problems and no one will be bold enough to talk to them.**

3. **Deposit your money or give your money to the chairperson before the deadline. Do not be one to be followed or reminded every time, it does not show integrity. Respect team members and deposit your money before others begin to get anxious wondering whether money is coming.**

4. Excuses and stories are a No ! No! , stories of funeral, sickness etc. We still contribute even in any of these circumstances otherwise you disrupt the whole group and the whole set up.

5. Do not ask to change positions or month you get your money. Stick to what you agreed on at the start. If you say you are ok being given in a certain month, do not start to change two months down the line.

6. Most important, pray for yourself and your team that God will provide the money and you will not disappoint each other. Money comes from God.

As a matter of fact, I thank God I have never been in a group with anyone who has defaulted. Not even once. That shows me that God is in it. Sometimes people including me just join by faith, but month after month the money comes. I have heard a lot of such testimonies. It's an action of faith. God provides the money.

We can have other groups of smaller amounts like $300, $200, $100 even $50 , it will help in meeting our targets as individuals and as a church.

As I write in America, we are preparing for the 2019 Talents. I already have a group set up of 20 people in the $1000 round and another one for $500.

It means about $30 000 will be given to God every month from just these few people not even talking of the entire church. That will take us a long way.

Remember we also have other business people who do not even need a team, but they are able to give these big amounts on their

6. TALENTS ROUNDS (MONEY CLUBS)

own.

It's called planning, and these are some of the strategies to work Talents.

Talents Oh Yeah!!

7. Good Godly Pressure When Working Talents

"For assuredly, I say to you, whoever says to this mountain, 'Be removed and be cast into the sea,' and does not doubt in his heart, but believes that those things he says will be done, he will have whatever he says."
Mark 11:23 NKJV

I have learnt that during Talents sometimes you declare something , some big figure, in faith and sometimes God will cause you to say out a number that you did not even plan to say but it will actually be God saying it through you or causing you to say it.

It was in 2005 and I was in Zimbabwe, my husband and I were District Pastors for Ruwa District. That time we had already been assigned to go to New Zealand, but we were still waiting for our visas.

It was a year of Talents. People that year had sort of started on a slow note. Inflation had hit our nation, and it was four years after we had gotten into millions. The million was now equivalent to slightly over a thousand US dollars I would say. That year everyone was talking of Millions because that is where we were. I will say this testimony using the equivalent of the million that time, which was 1 million - 1 thousand or slightly more than a

7. GOOD GODLY PRESSURE WHEN WORKING TALENTS

thousand. This will help those who never got into the world of millions to put value to my testimony and the amounts.

We had started well, and we were preparing on our first big day which was on the 20th March 2005. I do not forget this date because this big day was on my birthday.

I had been working hard and by that time, a week before the 20th I had worked about $5000 only and my target was $10 000 by the big day which was in a week's time.

We went to a national Council, it was a good meeting and at the end of the National Council I was asked to share a little bit on Talents. I was excited, as I always am about Talents.

I went up on to the podium. For those who do not know what a national council is, it's a board meeting for District pastors, Overseers and Bishops from the FIF churches all over Zimbabwe. This is a meeting for about 3 thousand leaders or more. Our Father and Mother were not there, they were away on missionary work.

People were clapping and happy as I went up the stage. We sang a Talents song and there was much excitement. As we finished the song and dancing, I began to encourage on Talents. It was fire fire because I had been given only 15 minutes.

As I was encouraging, I was excited, and in the excitement, (kuonererwa, manyemwe) I said, "we have a big day on Sunday and my husband and I are not going to give anything less than $20 000" Oh my God! Did I just say twenty thousand?? What have I done?

It was Tuesday and the Big day for Talents was in exactly 5 days. I had just hallucinated that I will have another $15 000 in 5 days' time.

People were surprised, challenged and shocked because up to

that time no one had been able to raise that amount yet. As I finished my short message and came down, many of the pastors came to me and told me they were so challenged and encouraged with my testimony and on Sunday they are sending teams to our church to witness our Big Day, so that they could take the fire back to their churches too. By the time we finished and were going to the car park more and more District Pastors were coming up to me and saying, either they would come with some of their leaders or they were sending a team to be at our Big day to catch the fire of Talents.

As we got into the car with my husband, Zenas, I was very sad. As we were driving home, I was giving these big sighs, very like a person under extreme pressure.

It caught my husband's attention and he caringly said to me " Are you ok, those sighs are not normal, are you in some pain of some sort?" I sadly answered, " I am under pressure because of that $20 000 I just talked about"

My husband said, " You know what? I think sometimes you over do these things, where on earth where you thinking you are going to get that kind of money in such a few days? Were you dreaming up there or what? Even me I wondered what you were talking about, because I know there is no way we can get that kind of money in such a few days. You are going to be embarrassed because all those people who have promised to come will come, and they will discover that you were lying about your figures." Oh my God! That was more pressure!

I became even more sad. Unfortunately, I could not even reverse that, I had already said it. Anyway, as we continued driving home, my husband just changed, he said " Anyway who knows, probably it is God who caused you to say that, be of good cheer, if it is God, he will cause you to have the money by Sunday".

7. GOOD GODLY PRESSURE WHEN WORKING TALENTS

That was better, it cheered me up a bit. At least my husband had now decided to agree with me in faith. Those kind of confessions will send you straight to the prayer closet. That night I did not sleep, I sneaked away into the lounge to pray and ask God for money. Some confessions are caused by God, but after the confession, nothing will happen unless we pray.

I was desperately in prayer, night and day and that week was a week of fasting as a church, we were fasting for our big Day. I went into desperate prayer and fasting. Even fasting day and night.
"Therefore, I say to you, whatever things you ask when you pray, believe that you receive them, and you will have them."
Mark 11:24 NKJV

Whatever things you say, when you pray, believe that you receive them, and you will have them. I believed as I prayed. I believed God for a miracle.

As I was praying, an idea came. A few weeks back, my brother Zephania had told me he was making a lot of money selling scrap metal in big quantities. Pressure brings us to our knees to pray and Prayer makes things happen.

I called my brother and enquired about the scrap metal. Yay, my brother was willing to do it for me. He told me that if I gave him a certain amount of money that was needed to hire a 5-tonne truck and also to buy the scrap metal from out of town, he would go get the scrap metal and we would supply to a Chinese business man who was buying the scrap metal.

I gave him the money and he went. That was on a Thursday and I had told him the dead line and he was supposed to be back by Saturday and we would deliver the metal on the same day. The Chinese guy would pay us cash for the scrap metal.

On the other hand, as I was waiting and praying for this order to come and the transaction to be successful, the Lord also impressed upon my heart to pray and encourage other people who had the potential to give big.

I called Mujuda, some of you know Mujuda from my other book, Change Your Measure. God had poured a spirit of giving in our church in Ruwa and God had caused his family to give away a house. The results of giving God a house were already beginning to manifest, because good things were happening in their lives.

The Lord impressed upon my heart to talk to them about the coming Big Day. I said to her, " God used you before to give big, and you made a difference to all the giving that was taking place in our City. May the same God use you again to make a difference to the giving that is going to take place on our Talents Big Day on Sunday"

She asked, "How much were you thinking, that we could give mama?"

I said, "One hundred thousand." I had hallucinated again! She was shocked, and she said , " Mum we do not even have that kind of money, we could try $10 000 but definitely not $100 000. So, I laughed and said to her, "You asked me how much and my faith is so big on you that I am believing $100 000 for you." At which she laughed and said , "It's just a wish mama but we do not have that kind of money."

Later on, she told me that after I spoke to her , she and her husband had no peace, they felt Godly pressure, which led them to prayer. They spent the whole day praying, crying to the Lord.

The following day on Friday, Mujuda and her husband Ralph

7. GOOD GODLY PRESSURE WHEN WORKING TALENTS

Mungwari came to our home in the afternoon. They were holding a bank cheque for 70 thousand dollars. The Lord had asked them to take money that they had invested for a project they wanted to do, they obeyed and that Sunday they gave 70 thousand. It was a Bang!!!!! For our Big day.

On the Saturday before the big day my brother called to say he was on his way coming with the scrap metal. He wanted to get to that Chinese guy before he closed his business at 5pm. I was praying, believing, because the big day was the following day.

Oh my God! My brother called and said the truck had broken down on the way. That was a big blow!! But I still believed it would happen. I told him to look for someone to fix it while I was praying this side. He did, and by the time the truck was fixed it was too late. The Chinese guy had closed his shop for the day. My brother said, "It will have to be Monday, no other way to do it."

I insisted, "Just come, call the Chinese guy and tell him you are on your way and he will have to open for you, so you can offload the truck."

Where there is a will, God makes a way.
"For if there is first a willing mind, it is accepted according to what one has, and not according to what he does not have."
II Corinthians 8:12 NKJV

He called the Chinese business man and he agreed to meet him at his business premise and offload the truck with his guys and pay for the consignment.

They offloaded around 12 midnight. I was waiting by the gate. My brother was paid for the consignment.

He was paid about $17 000. I gave him an appreciation, and by the next day, at the big day, I had $21 000 to give God.

I had been encouraging other people individually all this time. Among them was Elder Freddy Chimbare, who gave $20 000 on that day, Chinyembas, Rwodzis were all on $20 000. It was the doing of the Lord.

All the people who had promised to come or send their teams, surely did. By the time we got to church that day, the church building was already half way full of people from other Zaoga FIF churches, who had come to be stirred up by our giving.

On that day we raised 223 thousand as a church. There was so much joy and excitement. (Takanyatso onererwa zvedu) It was an amazing amount. No men can do these things unless the Lord is with him. We saw the hand of God. We were so happy, and that Sunday cannot be rubbed off from my memory.

"If you do well, will you not he happy."
Genesis 4 vs 7

The few names that I have mentioned above, have all moved from Ruwa. Some still attend church in Ruwa but all of them and many others were elevated by God and now own houses in the very up market low density suburbs, some of them have houses all over Harare. They are all now in the "Rich" category. You can never out give God.

We used to give God and confess that "One day, Ruwa will refuse us and we will go and live where the real people live" (kunogara vanhu) It was our joke as a church, but God has brought it to pass.

Even my husband and I were elevated, we now have a property, a house, a mansion in The Grange. This is one of the suburbs we always desired but never thought we would afford it. But through

7. GOOD GODLY PRESSURE WHEN WORKING TALENTS

working for God, God fulfilled the desires of our hearts. We completed building one wing, and its "Proper Proper Exquisite" and we are now finishing off the double storey wing. Just having a stand in that area and building a home in that suburb to me is a miracle. You will never go wrong with working for God and working Talents. It's the best way to change your measure.

Mujuda and her husband (Mungwaris) now own and run a school in Zimre Park named Ralph Junior School. They are doing very well. They own more than 20 mini buses and vans that ferry children to and from their door steps. God has truly blessed them, and they always say they have never regretted the grace of obedience that God gave them that year. Their 2 children are in Canada and both pay more than $30 000 per semester in school fees as International Students. That can only be the blessing of the Lord.

In the above testimonies, God gave me pressure to say a certain figure, that I would not have said in normal circumstances, but He Himself made it possible for it to happen.

Allow God to declare things through your mouth, do not reverse your words, just let it be. Believe and pray and God will make it happen.

Talents Oh Yeah! Unlock your miracles of a new business, a house, a car and abundance of finances through working Talents.

You can also unlock your miracle of healing, having children (if you are barren) many other miracles, read on , I will write about other people who have experienced miracles , in the following chapters and also have personal testimonies from individuals on how God changed their lives through working Talents.

8. Monthly Big Days- Appreciation

Usually when we work Talents, we set aside a day in a month that we call "A BIG DAY". A big day is a day that we plan as an assembly, a region or a province, to put our efforts together and give BIG.

Usually we can plan our Big days at the end of the month or first or second week of the following month. Here in the USA we usually do our big Day 2nd week of the following month. It was a request from some of us that they need a little time into the month before our Big day. We accepted it. As long as it works for all of us, we have no problem. Some do their big day right at the end of the month. No problem with that. Some beginning of the following month, all good.

Here in America, it means the January Big day is 2nd week of February, and we have big days every month in that order. We usually set all the dates for the Big days for that year and give them out to the churches so that people are well prepared, and they know the dates in advance.

Below is an example of Big days we have set for the 2019 Talents. We have already distributed to our churches together with the account numbers where all Talents money should be deposited. Talents money is not deposited into the local church account

8. MONTHLY BIG DAYS- APPRECIATION

but go straight into the Talents account. Of course, places are different, but this is what we are doing and encouraging here in the USA.

2019 USA NATIONAL CENTER TALENTS

BIG DAYS

January. 01/06/2019
  February. 02/10/2019
  March. 03/10/2019
  April. 04/14/2019
  May. 05/12/2019
  June. 06/09/2019
  July. 07/14/2019
  August. 08/11/2019
  September. 09/08/2019
  October. 10/13/2019
  November. 11/03/2019

Talents start in January and end in October. We finish working end of October. But our final Big day overlapped into November because of having our Big days a few days into the next month. We are all happy with that.

In our churches we should make a lot of noise about our Big Days (kutinhirisa). Do some flyers. Talk about it the whole month. Prepare for the Big Days spiritually and financially. When we plan to give BIG , God also plans to BLESS US BIG.

"But this I say: He who sows sparingly will also reap spar-

ingly, and he who sows bountifully will also reap bountifully."
II Corinthians 9:6 NKJV

If we give sparingly, leaving some aside, God will bless us sparingly. I have seen by experience that those who give God bountifully always reap bountifully.

The time of Big Days is a time to show off for your God. It's a time to prove who you are. It's a time to say, "I am the head and not the tail, above and never below, number one and not number 100 ha ha ha!!" It's a time to change your testimony, it's a time to make a difference in your assembly and in your church. It's a time to kill that Goliath and take away reproach from your church and from your assembly or your region, even your province or your nation. The church everywhere is looking for some little Davids who kill Goliaths!

"Then David spoke to the men who stood by him, saying, "What shall be done for the man who kills this Philistine and takes away the reproach from Israel? For who is this uncircumcised Philistine, that he should defy the armies of the living God?"
I Samuel 17:26 NKJV

At every church, I believe God raises a few people with great ability who are used by God to stir others up. You need a few like those for any church to excel.

There are people that I talk to individually. I ignite their fire individually. I encourage them as individuals and I also encourage the church. I believe they are people who are called just to support the work of God outstandingly and motivate others to give. In Dallas we have Elder Sizani Mhlanga , he calls himself a kingdom

8. MONTHLY BIG DAYS- APPRECIATION

Financier. He excels in all areas of giving. He gives outstandingly. In Ruwa I had Mujuda, in Christchurch, New Zealand I had Jeffrey Gohwa and in Boston I have Violet Gonzo, just to mention a few names.

Every church must have outstanding givers, not for the whole church to be on one level, like a hedge that is cut to the same size. If you are a leader, try to excel on your Big Day so you can lead by example. (shanda semunhu mukuru akatendwa naMwari) work like a big person that has been accepted and entrusted by God.

On big days we give incentives. In New Zealand we were giving badges to everyone who would give $1000+ at a big day. The next big day you wear all your badges (nyembe) showing who you are in the Lord and in the work of God. Sometimes we can give medals or trophies.

We also do positions. We can compile a list of the top 20 people. Everyone who is alive will one day or all the time desire to have their names appear on the top ten, top five or top twenty. It's all biblical, and its part of the Talents Vision.

Why would Paul talk to the Corinthian church about how the Macedonians had given? He was creating competition. Good competition where we prove each other unto love and good works.

"And let us consider one another in order to stir up love and good works."
Hebrews 10:24 NKJV

The vision of talents has aways been good, cheerful competition that brings encouragement and excitement, but even as we do that we must not lose the focus, we must not focus our giving on people but on God. What ever we do let us do it as unto the Lord.

Yes, it is allowed to stir up love and good works. Some people say :

"But when you do a charitable deed, do not let your left hand know what your right hand is doing,"
  Matthew 6:3 NKJV

I believe that as a church we are just one hand, either we are the right hand or the left hand, all of us. The other hand is the world outside. The Pharisees used to stand in the streets to display their good works and that was wrong. It must be inside our church, within our walls. As long as it's like that there is no problem. Paul went on to say , do not compare yourselves to yourselves, compare yourselves with someone else, that way , you are wise.

"For we dare not class ourselves or compare ourselves with those who commend themselves. But they, measuring themselves by themselves, and comparing themselves among themselves, are not wise."
  II Corinthians 10:12 NKJV

Paul says as long as your measure yourself with yourself you are not wise.

You need to hear and see what the next person is doing, hear what the other regions and provinces and even nations are doing. Sometimes you are just comparing yourselves with the next church in your area, but you are both doing very badly, you can both do better, get out of those boundaries and compare yourselves with those who are excelling, those who are alive.

Good, Godly, comparison. As for me I love being number One.

8. MONTHLY BIG DAYS- APPRECIATION

I do not want to be beaten, I do not want my church to be beaten. To me its number one or nothing. If at all I am beaten I do not take it lightly, I work even harder to accomplish great results. I fast and pray so that I can excel, and my church can excel. I just pray because money comes from God.

If you are a pastor, it's not good to lead a church that is always the tail. If you are an elder, it's embarrassing to be in a church that is always last. Pray , fast and give. Refuse to be ordinary as an individual and as a church.

I like to lead, but sometimes God raises some that I lead, they excel and surpass me, but I will be striving hard to do the best I can. God rewards every sacrifice. Some people just do not care . (chero zvazvaita) your blessings will also be (chero zvazvaita).

Set targets for your big day as a church. Encourage people to also set targets for themselves. The week into the Big Day must be a week of fasting. With me I never get into a Big Day without fasting and praying as a church. The week of the big day we usually fast from Monday to Friday and the last 3 days those who are able we do day and night or Valour. Valour is a nickname we gave to the day and night when we break our fast with soup only or just a cup of tea of course drinking a lot of water. Talents are spiritual. If we get into a big day while spiritually prepared, we get big results, if we get into a big day while in the flesh, being carnal, we will not hear the voice of God when he speaks, and we will not get big results.

"My sheep hear My voice, and I know them, and they follow Me."
John 10:27 NKJV

God speaks through the speakers of the word, He talks in your Spirit through the quiet voice and He talks through the word. If you are not prayerful you might miss His voice. He might be giving you a figure to believe on and believe God for provision, but if you are carnal you will think of what is surrounding you and might not hear His voice.

Let's give a lot of time to Talents during the big day. And that's when we announce all contributions. Like I said before, they are public funds and public funds must be announced publicly.

All the times we raised big amounts of money, we were praying and fasting. In Ruwa $223 000 in one day, we were fasting and praying that week, Christchurch $76 000 in one day, we were fasting and praying, Dallas $100 000 in one day, we were fasting and praying. Many other places and big days where we did outstandingly, it was only when we were fasting and praying.

If you are busy eating during the week into your big day, you cannot expect big results. Giving is deliverance from the spirit of poverty and that deliverance cannot take place unless we combine , prayer, fasting and giving.

"However, this kind does not go out except by prayer and fasting."
Matthew 17:21 NKJV

In my ministry I have seen with my own eyes, many people being completely delivered from poverty through giving. Better still when they combine the giving with prayer and fasting.

Talents Oh Yeah, unlock your miracle through working Talents.

9. Some Suggestions of Things We Can Do To Work Talents

"But we encourage you brethren, that you increase more and more, that you also aspire to lead a quiet life, to mind your own business, and to work with your own hands, as we commanded you, that you may walk properly toward those who are outside, and that you may lack nothing."
I Thessalonians 4:11-12 NKJV

In Talents we use our hands. We use our skills that God has given us, to do projects.

For me for 2019 Talents, I am using my gifting and skill to write books and that will be my main line of working, selling books and giving the money towards my Talents. I will do many other things, but this is the thing the Lord impressed on my heart for this season and I will still use the same skill and method for my home Talents. Jesus will first ask you for your boat to use it to preach to the people, after he has used it, he will say to you, **"Launch into the deep for a big catch."**

"Then He got into one of the boats, which was Simon's, and asked him to put out a little from the land. And He sat down and taught the multitudes from the boat. When He

had stopped speaking, He said to Simon, "Launch out into the deep and let down your nets for a catch." But Simon answered and said to Him, "Master, we have toiled all night and caught nothing; nevertheless, at Your word I will let down the net." And when they had done this, they caught a great number of fish, and their net was breaking."
Luke 5:3-6

There are many different things we can do to work Talents. In this chapter I will mention a few suggestions, some of these start small and can turn into big businesses. If you are already in a big established business, this might not be for you. You are already doing well. Continue with what you are doing.

Selling Food
- Tomatoes
- Onions
- Sweet potatoes

When I was working in a bank in Zimbabwe, I would always carry a box of the above in my car boot (trunk) . I would package them nicely in very neat plastic bags and price them, I would always supply to my work mates. Find a wise way to earn and get a share from your work mates earnings .Do not just live on your Salary only. You can do this with church Talents as well as home Talents.

Roasted Salted Nuts- buy raw dry nuts, roast and salt them in a pan. Package nicely and sell at any gathering, that is church etc. Even at work , tell them you are raising funds for a church project and this is your humble way to ask for donations.

In Dallas , I used to buy nuts, which were nicely packaged in

9. SOME SUGGESTIONS OF THINGS WE CAN DO TO WORK TALENTS

bottles. I would buy them from a grocery shop called Kroger and I would carry a basket of those nuts to church to sell them. I bought a bottle of nuts for $ $2.99 and sold them for $5.00.

Meat - Boreouvors, you can have this made at a butchery for a price and you put mark up.

Biltong- One can make biltong at home, but we need to strictly follow healthy regulations.

- You can make pies and samoosas and sell them.

- You can prepare meals for those who are too busy to cook and deliver the food. You advertise at church or by flyers. In developed nations this is a good business because some people want their traditional food like sadza but have no time to cook.

Catering business

You can start a catering business and advertise to cater for weddings, parties and meetings. Bake cakes for weddings and birthdays, and even just for selling to individuals .

Cleaning

You can start by cleaning for individuals, cleaning homes or offices etc.

This can grow until you have a big cleaning business. It can move from individuals into getting contracts with big companies to clean schools and offices.

My daughter and her husband own a prospering cleaning business in New Zealand . Shinah has a degree in Human

Resources and Mike her husband has a degree MBA. Both of them are now fully employed in their own cleaning business. They are doing very well, and this business started from the teachings in our church of encouraging people to do business and become entrepreneurs through working Talents.

Last year we visited them in New Zealand. On one of the days we went to the place they were cleaning with some workers in order to see how they were doing.

They were cleaning a big warehouse and they told us they had charged this company $10 000 for a five-day cleaning job. I mean, they won the contract and were going to take 5 days to clean that warehouse. We went to pray in the warehouse. After praying my husband asked how many square metres it was. Mike told us the square metres and then suddenly said he needed to remeasure the area. The company had told him it was so many square metres but he never bothered to check.

When they came back home after work, they were very happy. Mike had remeasured the place and he found out that the company had quoted less square metres than what was there. He consulted them, and they agreed to pay $17000 for that 5-day job. That is the doing of the Lord.

Do not despise the cleaning business. Its hard work but it pays very good.

Transport Business

Transport business can be simply operating a taxi business. If you can afford a vehicle you can have a taxi business.

In the USA, South Africa, Australia and UK there is Uber business. People are making a lot of money through Uber. You

9. SOME SUGGESTIONS OF THINGS WE CAN DO TO WORK TALENTS

need to have a car which is usually from 2007 and above (they want a good car). You should have a valid driver's license which has no bad record.

You can register with Uber and if accepted you download an App that you use . If you put the App on it will buzz if there is someone who needs to be picked in your area. You accept to pick them you are given the address and you go pick them and drop them where they are going. You do not handle any money except for tips (gratuity). The passenger pays directly to Uber through debit or credit card. You get your earnings weekly from Uber.

Some people make from $500 to $1000 a week. There is also Uber eats, where you just pick some food from a restaurant and deliver to the person who has ordered.

In USA there is lyft as well. It works exactly like Uber, it's just different companies. Food delivery (DoorDash, UberEats) has become very popular in the USA, especially in Texas.

Medical Transport

This is a very good business in the USA and I believe it could be in other countries too. This is where you get a contract to ferry patients to and from hospital. It could be some citizens who do not have transport. It is common with patients who need dialysis, they have to go to the hospital 3 or 4 times a week and some of them enjoy the benefit of medical transport. Obviously, there are a number of things they look at for one to qualify. The cars also must be good cars which are approved and covered by a very good insurance. If one get the contract. They might need to have a number of cars, up to twenty cars for this business but you can start with 3 to 4 cars. This can turn into a very big business.

The medical transportation business can also include carrying medical samples or medical supplies instead of patients.

There is also Amazon delivery, you sign up with Amazon and do 3 deliveries in a day for $60 if you are able to do more praise the Lord. In the USA if you search delivery business ideas, a lot will come out. Food delivery, eggs delivery, milk and bread delivery etc.

If you have a car, a valid license and you are not lazy, you can find something to do and all these businesses are flexible. You can do it whenever you are available or do it outside your normal working hours.

Selling Stuff on eBay

Talents taught me to sell stuff on eBay. I heard other ladies testifying on our Big Tuesdays. In the USA we do big Tuesdays once a month, on the conference call. All ladies will log in from the comfort of their homes. Sometimes we have more than a hundred women logging in. We started Big Tuesdays as a way to encourage each other on Talents. We then continued even after Talents. Many women look forward to our Big Tuesdays.

I heard some women saying , I am making up to a thousand dollars in a week and sometimes a day on eBay. I had no idea on how to set it up and I talked to some young ladies in our church in Boston. Jane Mugove and Rudo Mudzi tried to explain to me how to do it, I tried but me being Old School it was not so easy. One day Jane just surprised me, she came home to the Mission house and she told me God had assigned her to come help me set up my eBay business. She was amazing. She did everything. I went with her to Marshalls and TJ Marks where she showed me which bags we should buy, only designer bags will sell quickly on eBay, because there are people who specifically look for designer

9. SOME SUGGESTIONS OF THINGS WE CAN DO TO WORK TALENTS

bags and suitcases there. We buy things that are now on special, on a discount, reduced prizes, and we resell on Ebay for a profit.

We took pictures and posted them on my eBay account. Those bags were selling like hot cakes.

Someone was telling me you can also look for designer clothes in Goodwill shops (second hand shops) . Some are new and have labels on them and they sell very well on eBay.

Real Estate

This can also include being a Realtor. In America we call it Realtor but in other nations its Real Estate Agent. Do it properly, do the course and begin to sell houses. You might not sell a house every day but whenever you sell a house you get good money and big commission. You can get ten to twenty thousand dollars in one Sale.

In this category you can also do house flipping. Its whereby you buy dilapidated houses, old shabby houses, renovate them and sell them for a profit. In most cases this can bring very good profits. You can buy a house for $25 000, use another $20 000 or $25 000 to renovate it and sell it for $80 000 to $90 000. If you do not have enough capital, team up with one or two faithful friends and give it a go.

Day Care

You can look after kids at home for a fee. In America there is also adult day care where people also leave their aged parents with someone to take care of them during the day.

Using Your Skill or Profession to make Money

This one is most common. If you are a doctor, a nurse, caregiver, teacher, designer, radiologist, pharmacist you can use your profession either to establish your own practice or alternatively just pick extra shifts and work for the Lord. I know someone who is a nurse who worked $60 000 in ten months through just working extra shifts. If your scheduled duty is 3 days a week, why not do Monday through Friday and work the extra 2 days as extra shift.

You can also pick those shifts when we do home talents and you can save for a house or something big.

If you are a teacher, you can do extra lessons right in your home and earn a lot of money.

If you are a designer do web designs for companies. My son Emmanuel made a lot of money in New Zealand doing web design for companies as a side job.

I met a doctor recently, an Elder in our church, a medical doctor in South Carolina, Dr Mazaiwana. He was so excited about the upcoming Talents and told me he was going to use his profession and skill to work for God. He was setting up a business in the line of his profession.

A lot more people especially in Dallas have gone into home care business. They set up a home and are able to take care of some old people and they get good money even for a minimum of 3 people in a house.

Cross boarder Trading

This is very common in Africa. People go to South Africa, Zambia, Tanzania, America; UK, Turkey to order some merchandise for resale. This could be clothes, jewelry, hand bags and a lot

9. SOME SUGGESTIONS OF THINGS WE CAN DO TO WORK TALENTS

more.

Many people say you cannot go wrong with selling food and women's stuff. People eat, and they need food again the following day. Women never get tired of buying some beauty supplies and this too is a good business line.

Hair and Face Products for Women

A business that is very easy to run is to sell hair products, face products for women. Hair plaiting also goes into this category. You just need a little training and you can plait or sow on a weave. I remember when people started to have these weaves. The hairdressers were charging a lot of money to do a weave on. I went to have my hair done, I looked at how this lady was doing it and I saw that it was simple, I could do it. And then I offered to do a weave on a friend for free. I did it so well that through her I got many customers. Every day after work I would be fixing someone's hair and got some good money.

My daughter too Diana Blessing made a lot of money plaiting some hair when she was in UK. When she was in college studying to be a Radiographer, she made a lot of extra money through plaiting hair. I could not recall her doing a course on hair plaiting and when I asked her, she said she learnt it when she was young as they plaited their dolls with her young sister Shinah and her cousins, then they started to plait each other's hair and she just polished up her skills when she was in UK.

Gardening and Poultry

In Zimbabwe many people make a lot of money through farming, gardening and poultry.

Some people just specialize in vegetable farming, green houses and they supply big Supermarkets.

Some do poultry, rearing some chickens for resale and some hens for eggs and selling the eggs. I know some people who have up to 2000 or 3000 chickens at a time.

The best is to find information on the project you want to do. Talk to the people who are doing it.

In Talents we encourage that you do not hide information from others because the money is going towards one cause. As long as the person is not targeting your clients, give them information. Also, it's not everything that one can do, even as you read these suggestions , there are some suggestions that will jump up and excite you and you feel you want to do it. Other suggestions do not even raise a little interest in you. Leave them, they are not for you. Even if something jumps up to you and you get excited about wanting to do it, a lot of prayer is still needed until you feel a confirmation in your heart.

Let's also promote each other's business and buy from each other. Children can be encouraged to sell chocolates, cookies and candies (lorries, sweets).

Sometimes just buy from someone for the sake of just encouraging them. You might not really need what they are selling, how many times have I gone into a Supermarket and bought some things that I did not really need, and that money was gone for good. How many times do I buy some food that I end up throwing away because I do not like it and that money is gone for good and forever, but tell you what, everything you do for Christ will last and you will get a reward if you faint not.

Buy some nuts from that old lady who is making an effort to work for God, encourage her. Buy something from that young lady who is putting all her effort to work for God, she needs encouragement.

9. SOME SUGGESTIONS OF THINGS WE CAN DO TO WORK TALENTS

I passed through our Maryland church in the USA. The ladies are all geared for 2019 Talents. They have agreed that every woman can sell some grocery item and they buy from each other. Even their children will sell small things like candy etc. I really liked the unity in Maryland. I am sure they will do well in the 2019 talents.

Let's learn to buy from each other, to promote each other's business.

Let us all go at once and begin to work Talents. Do not be left out in what God is doing in this season. Create a reason for God to bless you.

Your miracles are in these Talents, your breakthrough is in working Talents. Do not ignore Talents.

Talents Oh Yeah!!!

10. Testimonies of Miracles After Working Talents

I have heard thousands of testimonies of people whose lives completely changed after working Talents. Talents is the best way to tap into the Blessing of the Lord that makes rich and adds no sorrow with it.

"The blessing of the Lord makes one rich, And He adds no sorrow with it."
Proverbs 10:22 NKJV

A blessing is not only money, but a blessing is all round, good health, peace, joy , prosperity and provision is also part of a blessing. Blessed home and away. Your children blessed. Your grandchildren blessed. I can testify to this. I know very well some of the blessings my children enjoy are not from what they have done but from what we have done, causing my descendants to be blessed up to the fourth generation. If you do not work for God , you are cruel to your children and grandchildren, they will struggle in life.

One of my grandchildren at ten years old was earning $25 per hour as an actor for children's programs in Australia. Every time the mother, my daughter would accompany her, she would also be paid $25 per hour. That is what I call , a blessing. She has stopped

10. TESTIMONIES OF MIRACLES AFTER WORKING TALENTS

doing it now because the parents want her to concentrate on her studies, but God has given her a lot of skill in that area.

God educated all my children, they never struggled. One has a degree in Radiology, (her husband also a radiographer and now holds a managerial position) . They are in Australia and they already have a house there, they are not renting. The next one has Human resources and International business degree and has worked as an HR manager in New Zealand. Now, together with her husband run a successful cleaning business, and my daughter is using her skills to employ staff and run payrolls at their business. The husband has an MBA degree. Recently they told me they had managed to save $80 000 as a deposit for a house they are in the process of buying. That surely is a sign that God is blessing them. I apologise leaking all their secrets here, but it's my testimony of what God can do if parents choose to work for God.

Our only son Tatenda has a diploma in Sound Engineering and another Diploma in Information Technology, he currently works as an IT Engineer in New Zealand. He is still growing up and learning life but the most important thing that I know is he is blessed. Remember he is the one who was once blessed with two cars in one day when he was only seventeen years old (testimony in my book. Change your measure).He is carrying a blessing and blessings will always follow him.

My adopted daughter Natasha has graduated with a degree in Psychology and is studying Masters in the same field. She loves the Lord, is very prayerful, rents her own apartment, drives a nice car and her future is very bright. I have no complain when it comes to my children's blessings and my only prayer for them is to also excel in the things of God.

I just want to give some wisdom to someone. Just work for God and he will take care of your children and grandchildren.

Below I will pick on a few testimonies of people who experienced blessings and miracles after working for God. I have included individual testimonies not only from the USA, but other countries like Australia, New Zealand, UK, and South Africa. Talents made a difference in their lives and in the lives of many other people who I could not all include in this book.

I believe these testimonies will encourage you to also work for the Lord and make a difference.

Miracles of Prosperity

"There is one who scatters yet increases more; And there is one who withholds more than is right, But it leads to poverty."
Proverbs 11:24 NKJV

The above proverb is very true when it comes to working Talents. During the time of Talents people give as if they have no care, as if they have no needs of their own, they put their own needs aside and concentrate on giving God. For ten months people give cheerfully.

Here is what Solomon noted among his people during his time. The ones who scattered increased even more. Another version says, one person gives freely, and they get richer, another says one person is more generous and they become wealthier and another withholds what they are supposed to give, and it leads to poverty.

Talents is the time to give freely so you can become richer or you can increase financially, or you become wealthier.

What Solomon noted amongst his people, I have also noted

among my people as a pastor. The people who get excited about Talents and give according to their ability are blessed and I have seen them , all of them , become better and better financially and in life. Those who ignore Talents, some even choose to stop coming to church during the time of Talents, this group become poorer and poorer, they are the most borrowers ,they borrow and struggle to pay back or not even pay back, they struggle financially, most in this group are not even faithful tithers. Sometimes you can easily tell that this person does not participate in what others do for the Lord by the way their life is so miserable, no progress in life. Life is a dilemma.

Talents testimony
Debra and Noreel Boston USA

Let me mention a woman I met in the Boston church a few years ago. Her name is Debra. She is proud of her testimony and she does not mind me writing about it.

Apostles E.H. Guti and E. Guti went to plant a church in Boston in 2015. Their first fruit was this lady and her husband Noreel. They were very poor and homeless. 4 children taken by the government (DCF). Debra was living in a shelter. She would walk with a satchel which had all her belongings, that was all, because in the Shelter in the USA you are just given a place to sleep and, in the morning, you take your everything and go, and you come back in the evening to sleep. You do not go to the same bed or same room you were the previous day, so one cannot keep anything there.

They accepted Jesus Christ as their personal savior, that alone is a big miracle of being taken from death to life, from eternal destruction to eternal life. I am going to concentrate of what happened when she started giving God.

Baba Guti did not just give them Jesus, but he helped them financially here and there, for their transport and other needs. It was no job, no money and no permanent abode situation.

My husband and I were assigned to shepherd that church after the apostles left. The people were full of love and showed Debra and her husband a lot of love and always helped them financially. We would always make sure we give them some money for transport and other things, so they could continue to be able to come to church. Debra faithfully attended church.

"If a brother or sister is naked and destitute of daily food, and one of you says to them, "Depart in peace, be warmed and filled," but you do not give them the things which are needed for the body, what does it profit? Thus, also faith by itself, if it does not have works, is dead."
James 2:15-17 NKJV

One day as she was leaving church, I called her back and I said to her, "I just called you back because I want to give you something". I took $20 from my purse to give her and she said, "Do not worry mama, someone just gave me some money, it will be enough for now, you can give me some other day." I was surprised. She is refusing money. It means she is not enjoying this "being given"life.

The next incident that surprised me, was the first day I ever talked about giving. I was talking to the women after church, we were planning for our Sister to Sister Luncheon. After giving my own contribution towards this function, I asked the women to also contribute, those who were able. To my surprise, as others were contributing, Debra pulled out her purse and I saw her taking out a creased $20 note and also giving like everybody was

10. TESTIMONIES OF MIRACLES AFTER WORKING TALENTS

doing. I was impressed. No one was ever expecting her to give. We all understood that she did not have, but she chose to give. Everyone right there was surprised, I could see everyone's look.

You know what? It's easy to allow people to sympathize with your poverty and you get more poorer and poorer, but the best is to choose to get out of poverty by giving.

From that time every time we gave to God, she would also give.

About 4 months later, we started to work Talents, 2016 Zegu Talents. Debra kept on saying she was looking for a job because she wanted to work Talents.

God gave her a job. She was not earning much, but she now had a live-in job, that meant, food and accommodation for her and a little money at the end of the month.

Not long after she just surprised us by giving $1000 towards Talents. $1000 ??? the secretary called me literally crying. Debra of all people had given $1000. I called her, just to encourage her and also as her pastor I was concerned whether she was left with something.

Her answer surprised me, she said: her job had actually finished that day, she was only supposed to receive $400 but the boss had surprised her by saying he was now taking his mum to an old people's home, but his mother had told him that Debra took very good care of her, so he was giving her slightly above $1000. She said she knew it was a miracle because she has been praying for some money to give to Talents, sowing for a better life and for her children to be released back to her one day.

She told me not to feel pity for her because this was the only way for her life to change. She said, I listened to all you teach on giving and I am going to do it. I want God to change my life", she said.

God being the faithful God that he is, the following week Debra got a job where she was earning $25 per hour, working 12 hour shifts per day.

There is one who scatters and yet increases even more, she was earning like a qualified nurse.

That was the beginning of a changed life. As I write about 3 years later, Debra and Noreel now has a rented home of their own, 4 bedroomed home, where they pay $1 800 a month. A home of their own!!! That alone is a big miracle. Remember they were homeless, obviously no credit history to help them get a home, but God is good, just them getting a house with no credit history is a big miracle. We are all believing their children will be released soon. They have been battling for them in the courts , God has been on their side, and we all know God gave them the accommodation so that the children will all fit in the four bedroomed home. She is very faithful in her tithing. As I speak, she is one of the candidates in the $1000-dollar round for the 2019 Talents. We serve a faithful God.

I have a lot of testimonies of people who have been prospered through working Talents. Their lives completely changing after they begin to work Talents.

My Talents Testimony- A blessed Life

My husband and I are a testimony of what God can do when we chose to live a life of giving. We have seen God uplifting us in life and financially. We have seen ourselves being able to achieve or afford things we never thought we would ever achieve in life. There is a life we never ever thought we would live, cars we never thought we would ever drive, a house in an area, we

10. TESTIMONIES OF MIRACLES AFTER WORKING TALENTS

never imagined we could live, furniture we never ever thought we could afford, monies we never thought we could ever hold. God has been faithful, and to us to work Talents is a joy and an opportunity never to be missed.

I believe that for God to send us to New Zealand with our children was part of our blessing of working for the Lord. I am not saying those who did not get such an opportunity are not blessed, but our blessings differ according to what plans God has for us. That assignment brought about the blessing of better schools for my children and we never struggled with School fees because of the opportunities available overseas.

From New Zealand to the USA for me and my husband, I also see the grace and blessing of the Lord. It's good to appreciate God for what we have. I do not take it lightly.

Talking about financial blessings that come after working Talents, let me give you this testimony. After the last Talents, 2016 Zegu Talents, we received a financial blessing as soon as we finished.

We had an investment home that we bought while we were in New Zealand. When we got transferred from New Zealand, we decided to sell the property because it would be hard to manage it while we were far. When we made the necessary enquiries, we discovered that we were going to make a loss on it. We were going to remain with a debt. We decided to leave it like that and let it continue paying itself. Tenants paying the rent and the rent servicing the mortgage. We checked on the value many times and we were still going to have a loss if we sold it. It had not appreciated in value.

A miracle happened soon after the 2016 Zegu Talents. Our Son in law Michael, called my husband and said "Dad do you still want to sell your house? Houses in your area have shot up in prices. The Chinese people are buying houses cash in that area and there is a great demand" my husband answered " Really? Do you think we can get as much as $20 000 on top of the value of the house?" Michael said, " even $50 000 daddy, just put it on the market for a crazy amount and see what happens."

We surely did, we put it on the market for $400 000 when its value was $300 000. It was sold within some weeks. We made NZ $100 000 profit on our house. After they took out their charges, we made a straight $85 000 into our pockets. This is the first time ever to hold such an amount of money. It went a long way into the project we are doing in Zimbabwe ,we are building a mansion, a double storey beautiful home.

We had stopped the project to work talents, gave $21 000 for Talents and immediately reaped $85 000. That was not a coincidence, these are some of the blessings that follow after working Talents.

By the way, ladies in the USA have nicknamed me "Mama Proper Proper exquisite" I love classy things it gives glory to my God.

It was also soon after working Talents that we were blessed with cows in New Zealand (full story in my book, Change your measure). 10 commercial milk cows insured at $3000 a cow. We were just given commercial cows, milk cows, as a gift by someone we had known just for a few days. They said God had told them to give us the cows.

It was soon after working Talents that God made it possible for us to buy land (a stand) in The Grange in Harare Zimbabwe. It was soon after Talents that we finished the guest wing and furnished it, proper proper exquisitely. Home Talents for 2017 we bought all the furniture or most of the furniture for our main

10. TESTIMONIES OF MIRACLES AFTER WORKING TALENTS

house that we are finishing now. All furniture for that house is already there, and its proper proper. We are putting the project aside for now, so we do the 2019 Talents and I know soon after, it will be easy to finish off that mansion. I have seen by experience that God intervenes in our projects if we intervene in his projects.

I have looked back in my life and seen that most of the major developments we have done or achieved in life has been soon after working Talents.

"**Or who has first given to Him And it shall be repaid to him?**"
Romans 11:35 NKJV

When God repays, it will be pressed down, shaken together and running over. Blessings that you will not be able to contain.

Miracles of Entrepreneurship

<u>Talents Testimony from</u>
Pastor Gertrude Mageza Boston USA

Below is a testimony from Gertrude Mageza. One of the ladies who challenged me on why I was not telling them about Talents, in Boston. She and her husband Robert Mageza have only worked Talents once, 2016 Zegu Talents.

The Lord has done so much for the family in these past 3 years or 2 years after the Talents. Here is her testimony in her own words.
"In 2015 our family started a small carpet business out of our home which didn't make a lot of money. As we were working the ZEGU 2016 miracle talents God gave us ideas and the ability

to expand our business portfolio to increase our revenue stream. We experienced a miracle because one of the businesses grew and we had to move into an industrial park, employed 10 people and that year we were surprised as it made a gross revenue of $877,000 before tax and expenses in 2016.

The school of Talents taught us to continue with our entrepreneurial spirit and in 2017 we ventured into real estate investment. We had a few startup hiccups, but in mid-2018 as we continued to sow into the Kingdom of God – we have seen the hand of God. Our real estate portfolio has now grown into 12 houses here in the United States of America. I remember in late October closing the sale on 3 houses in one day. That is a miracle!!

If it wasn't for Talents, we would not have diligently pursued entrepreneurship as much as we did with as much zeal. My family recognized the covenant and Spirit behind it – to get us out of poverty. Obstacles are from the devil and are seen as stepping stones to our goal I believe that in working 2019 Talents God will do more miracles."

Gertrude Mageza and her husband Evangelist Robert Mageza worked more than $12 000 in 2016, and it is amazing what God has done in this short time. Running over blessings.

Talents Testimony
Elder Sam and Lizzie Mutizwa Dallas Texas USA

It was in 2012 when I decided to diversify from one business

10. TESTIMONIES OF MIRACLES AFTER WORKING TALENTS

into Medical Transportation services, I applied for a contract with Texas dept of Health Services (HHSC). I felt in my spirit that God had given me that contract, 2012 went by and came 2013 no contract, I am a giver by nature I give to the work of God I pay my tithe and the men of God around me knew it and often reminded God of the good things I did, yes I listened to those prayers and agreed with them all the way and my God is faithful I never lacked He supplied me with all my needs, but the one thing I really desired to have was that transportation business and I was not getting my breakthrough.

I was beginning to lose hope and getting impatient my Overseer Dr Cathy could see it in the spirit, so she came to me after 21 days of fasting and praying and she said and I quote "you have done everything but now I want you to change your measure of giving I want you to do talents and I want you to do big, when you want God to do what he has not done in your life, you need to do what you have never done before. Work outstandingly in these Talents and provoke God ".

We started the talents In February and in the 3rd month of 2014 I started taking from my savings 4th month and 5th went by and at the end of the 6th month I received an offer letter for that transportation business I was believing for and sowing for contract was effective 09/01/2014, Glory to God, he is very faithful.

Now I didn't have enough money to buy the minimum 10 vehicles required by the state for me to be accepted as a vendor. When I presented my 5 vehicles they were excited to have me and allocated me an area that only required 5 vehicles, now that area is one of the biggest in the region and I now have 18 cars. I have 18 drivers, 2 dispatchers and 3 CNA. Thanks to Talents.

That year by God's grace I worked $23 700. I had never worked such a big amount before, I do not regret because from 2014 my businesses have flourished.

The God of Ezekiel through the school of talents has brought my family out of darkness, I was totally delivered from the spirit of regression, spirit of going round and round financially. I now know what it means to live in financial abundance. Besides transportation company we now have assisted living homes and a small car dealership that we are believing will shoot up after the 2019 Talents. Looking forward to more miracles after working 2019 Talents.

Talents Woyee!!!!

Talents Testimony
Elders Tinos & Jescah Masaka AUSTRALIA NSW

I'm thankful to the God of our Father Ezekiel Guti who ushered us to the life changing school of Talents. Though I started working Talents as a Youth, it was in 2006 while in New Zealand where we learnt the true meaning of Talents. In 2008 after we relocated to Australia, the Lord enabled us to give $25000 towards Talents by cleaning a Day-Care Centre together with my wife after hours. Not long after, the Lord opened another stream of income through a contract worth over $80 000 for my Engineering Consultancy business which also provided free accommodation for a year.

A couple years later we embarked on working the ZEGU Talents, we set a target to raise $50000, prayerfully I distributed

10. TESTIMONIES OF MIRACLES AFTER WORKING TALENTS

business cards for our cleaning company – Kingdomclean and got a contract to clean 100 houses. We received a total payment equal to our target and we faithfully and joyfully gave the whole amount to God. The cleaning business birthed from the Talents school continued such a few months later, we were able purchase in one full payment of $42000, a stand in Mt Pleasant Heights, Zimbabwe where we are building a beautiful double story house. Through the same cleaning business, we gave another $50000 on the Talents that followed and through this grace of giving, God recently opened us yet another stream of income through recruitment of international students.

KINGDOM FINANCIER THROUGH SCHOOL OF TALENTS.
Elder Sizani and Ruwa Mhlanga Dallas Texas USA

I relocated to USA in 2004 and from 2004 to 2008 l had been working call center jobs ..having trained as an engineer l was never satisfied with my earnings l felt there was more to life ..l remember a time in 2008 when l got retrenched and soon after being retrenched l got hurt and was bedridden for three months and at some point l was homeless…after my recovery end of 2008 l remember borrowing $4 000 from my sister to open a tax preparation office .

This is a business centered on numbers and there is so much competition from big companies dominating the industry. I remember my pastors teaching me at that time as they came to pray for my business that create a reason for your blessing . I decided to partner with God by giving towards ministerial needs. l remember that year 2009 making ridiculous pledges that got me into a depression thinking where l was going to get that money. There were times l would start crying as l prayed going to my office saying to God where will l get this money that l pledged if you don't give me customers. It was not looking good for me that year, but l remember reminding God through His scriptures about His promises regarding talents that God was going to bless the works of our hands through working talents to support His work. Every morning as I walked into my office l would prophesy greatness to my business based on the partnership contributions.

That year l broke even and with the money I made I honored my promises to God. I thought of quitting, but something told me He is a faithful God and Mwari haadye chemunhu. He is a covenant keeping God. l declared to myself l would see the hand of the Lord in the land of the living...the following year l saw my clientele doubling and that's when l realized the hand of the Lord was upon my business because there is so much competition in the business it's not easy to grow. From that year it became a pattern of doubling every year. Today our clientele is over 3000 customers and it's a miracle to have such a number in this business. Every year we are receiving offers from the big companies surrounding us wanting to buy us out because they are being threatened by our rapid growth .Only because of this God. The years that we work talents are the years that we have seen big jumps in our numbers . Talents have taught me how to plead my case and put God in a corner regarding business expansion. It's as if l have a platform to stand on to declare my needs before Him because there is a covenant behind them. In the last two talents we worked 50k and the second year we worked 37k. Our biggest secret is giving towards talents , giving towards missions to the servant and apostle of God.

In 2018 we gave over 25k towards missions to the apostle of God and then we also support missionary work in other nations and in addition we also support our local pastors. I can tell you that when you culture a habit of giving consistently before God there is a time that comes where you bump into blessings left right and center. When I sowed into the life of the servant and apostle this year I said to that seed that this year I need to expand internationally.

When I left for Zimbabwe God opened a door with the top leadership of the nation in the area of mining. That was something I never dreamt of happening in my life but because of His grace and working for Him it happened and there is a big testimony coming out of that venture .Through working talents the God of Ezekiel also blessed us with finances to build a multimillion-dollar home debt free in Zimbabwe something that we never thought we could afford if it wasn't for His covenant with our father. I have so many testimonies that are loading that I believe I will be able to share in the next year or two because of working talents.

I call myself a Kingdom Financier and that's who I am, School of Talents has made it possible for me to be financially Useful to the Kingdom of God.

MIRACLE OF BUYING A HOUSE ON CASH AFTER WORKING TALENTS Testimony
Elders Kurumbidza and Josi Chani - Phoenix Arizona USA

God has been good. We have seen the hand of God in our lives through working talents. Both my husband and I were born in FIF. We used to participate in magaba when we were Sunday school kids. My family came to the US in the early 90s. When the church started in the US, we were told that we would start working talents and we were so excited about the opportunity.

I started working talents on my own as a youth kid. After getting married my husband came from Zimbabwe and we started work together. I remember one year as we were working talents, we felt that we needed to sell one of our personal cars to raise money for talents. We sold our car and that year we worked about $15000 in talents.

We began to see God doing miracles in our lives. I had school loans worth $12000. We were able to pay the loans off within a year. We also paid off a car loan which we had at the time. After some time, God blessed us with a used car business. All the cars we have we've purchased with cash. In 2015 we got the opportunity to work home talents and we purchased our house for cash, buying a house for cash in America. Through the used car business, we were able to start a car leasing business for uber/Lyft drivers where we started building a small fleet of cars. God is so good. We have seen that the covenant which he gave to us through his servant Baba Guti is at work in our lives. And greater things are still to come.

MIRACLES OF HEALING

Besides the financial blessing, I have seen and witnessed people who got their miracles of healing after working Talents or working for God, giving to the work of God.

We have testimonies of people like Mai Zakeo, well known in our church for working Talents. She was diagnosed of cancer in her old age and God healed her. Our father always says she was healed because of living a life of Giving. She created a reason for God to bless and heal her.

10. TESTIMONIES OF MIRACLES AFTER WORKING TALENTS

Our father Apostle E. H. Guti always teaches that people who work for God, give to the work of God are blessed with long life.

"Then Peter arose and went with them. When he had come, they brought him to the upper room. And all the widows stood by him weeping, showing the tunics and garments which Dorcas had made while she was with them. But Peter put them all out and knelt down and prayed. And turning to the body he said, "Tabitha, arise." And she opened her eyes, and when she saw Peter she sat up. Then he gave her his hand and lifted her up; and when he had called the saints and widows, he presented her alive. And it became known throughout all Joppa, and many believed on the Lord."
Acts 9:39-42 NKJV

Tabitha was given more life because of good works. Make a difference in your life by working Talents.

MIRACLES OF HEALING, GIVEN LIFE AGAIN!
Violet Gonzo- Boston, USA

My testimony is really simple. When Baba came to open a FIF church in Boston it was a prayer answered for me. (Earlier that year I had been diagnosed with stage 4 was esophageal cancer and given 3 weeks to live)

I was so ecstatic that I needed to catch up with my tithes. I didn't realize that one of the pastors who had come with Baba and Mama noticed and told them. She also told them about my diagnosis. Right away Baba, Mama, Overseers George and Rudo Rwizi laid hands on me and prayed. Later on, Baba assured me that what I was going through was just a process and that I was healed.

He told me the story of Mbuya Zakeo how after she was healed, she dedicated her life to working for the Lord. Viscerally my perception of Baba's wisdom took root.... there was no looking back. I was still getting chemotherapy and radiation, but I never missed a day from work. Some patients who were receiving the treatment as me died but I just knew that God was sparing my life for a purpose. Paying tithes or contributing to our new church was only the beginning then came Zegu.

Although Doctors had a very bad prognosis for me (Cancer had spread to other parts of my digestive system) I focused on the covenant that baba made with his God and my job as a child is to be obedient. So, I set a goal and worked Zegu Talents. Note, this was my first time working talents as an adult. The only other time I ever worked any talents was "Magaba" when I was little girl. I do remember my mom working talents growing up BUT this time she was the cheer leader with encouragement. Under the tutelage of Overseer Cathy, the rest is history. I worked 60 thousand dollars on the Zegu Talents and by God's grace I was No 1 in America, from there I just give God wholeheartedly and outstandingly in all areas Missions, Multi-Purpose, love offering, name it. I am geared up for 2019 Talents. Just the fact that I am alive and leaving a normal life is a big Miracle.

My healing is still in progress BUT my purpose in giving and working for the Lord with all my heart will remain my focus. God has blessed me every time I give/donate/contribute.

MIRACLE OF HEALING- RESTORATION OF SIGHT.
ESTHER CHIHOTA (QUEEN ESTHER)- Atlanta Georgia, USA

10. TESTIMONIES OF MIRACLES AFTER WORKING TALENTS

There is God in heaven who sees your works and rewards. I am one of the people who has been working Talents in our Church. Each time Talents were declared, I got excited. I would work Talents with all my heart. I would bring every penny that I worked to God.

At one time I worked $5 000.00 and when we were building ZEGU, I worked $10 000.00 These are not the only Talents I have worked. There was no time that I did not work Talents. I didn't want to be left behind because there are rewards in working Talents, there are Spiritual and Physical rewards/benefits when you work Talents with a willing heart.

God gave me Physical reward by healing my physical body. I got ill unexpectedly, which almost took away my life. People in my church are witnesses to this.

My vision was affected. I could not go to work. I had no income. The whole situation changed my life to the extent of losing memory. My daughter was the one who drove me everywhere. Her schedule changed to suit mine, doctors' appointments, church etc. God bless my daughter.

I was being prayed for. I got healed and improved a lot, but my eyesight was still a big issue/problem. I still couldn't drive.

I went back to work. My daughter was still driving me. At this time, it was work, doctors' appointments, church etc. You can imagine my daughter did not have a life of her own. I was part of her daily schedule.

In 2018, Overseers Dr Cathy and Dr Zenas came to Pastor our Church Assembly for a short time.

One day when ladies were in a Tuesday Morning Prayer Meeting, Dr Cathy prayed for me and prophesied to me. She said "God is going to heal your eyesight. You will be able to see well and be able to drive yourself". When they left and went back, I got my eyesight back. I began to drive on my own, day or night, rainy, cloudy and foggy day. The prophesy was confirmed. Glory to God!! I am totally healed, and have my sight back.

God remembered my works of working Talents, faithfully, willingly and bringing all the money to God. Those Talents that I worked, I got a physical reward, healing of my body and restoring my eyesight.

I advise and encourage people to work Talents. They are spiritual. Whenever Talents are called for, work together with others. There will be an anointing in those Talents for that season. Breakthroughs, healings, deliverance, miracles of any kind are in working Talents. Sometimes you do not need laying on of hands. Your answer could be in working Talents willingly and bringing all the money to God. It is all for your benefit.

God sees. He remembered me and rewarded me by healing me. Talents Oh Yeah!!!!

Miracles of Children

Twins Elders Haku (Hupenyu) and Thoko- Australia

I would like to specifically talk about this couple Haku (Hupenyu) and Thoko. I have written about them in my book (Change your measure) I am writing about them again because their testimony is specifically on Talents. They are now in Australia, but this happened while they were in New Zealand.

Hupenyu and Thoko had one child who was ten years old.

10. TESTIMONIES OF MIRACLES AFTER WORKING TALENTS

Hupenyu and Thoko were elders in our church in Christchurch, New Zealand. Hupenyu had been healed of leukemia. After going through the chemotherapy, he was told by the doctors he will not be able to have children again. Whose report are you going to believe???

He and his wife definitely did not accept the doctor's report. They came to us as pastors and asked us to pray for them, because they wanted twins and are believing God for twins. We prayed with them and we also advised them to sow a seed for the twins. We were just going into a year of working Talents. We told them to sow for their twins. We also announced to the church that we should no longer call them by their names, but we should call them Father and Mother of Twins (Baba naMai Matwins).

They worked very hard in the 2008 Talents. They worked more than $12 000 . Every month we were giving badges to those who worked $1000 and above. People would wear their badges on our Big Days. Hupenyu and Thoko gave more than $1000 every month and got a badge, but I never saw them wearing any of the badges.

When I asked them why they were not wearing their badges, they told me that they had set up a room for the twins and they were pinning the badges on the twins clothes. They meant business and they were serious about it.

After finishing the Talents, Thoko was pregnant. And guess what? It was twins! No history of twins from both families, but they worked Talents sowing for twins and they got them. God gave them the twins they sowed for.

The twins Tawanzwanashe and Isheunopa a boy and a girl, will be 9 years in 2 months.

There in Christchurch a number of families got their miracles of children (more details in change your measure).

I do not know what miracle you are believing God for? It could be financial? Or a house, a car or your business to be prospered, or is it starting a new business, a you are believing God for a husband or a wife. Are you 35 years and above and nothing has been happening in the line of marriage. I have helped a lot of girls in this category and they got their miracles. Let me share Miriam's testimony.

MIRACLES OF MARRIAGE Talents Testimony
Elder Miriam Flores- NEW YORK, USA

I was Born Miriam Sithole Musiwa, but God changed my name as he did that of Jacob after a fight with an angel. Even though my fight was not with an angel of the lord in the wee hours of the morning; it was with generational curses in my blood line. Thank God for giving us shepherds after his own heart who are gifted in different aspect of the ministry. When Dr Catherine Marurama stepped in to our region few years ago, God changed my life in short amount of time through her ministry of giving.

It is during this Time I fell in love with raising money for the kingdom of God through working Talents. Even though I had worked Talents in the prior years, this time it was different. I had a different understanding and I needed to go to another level by changing my measure . Dr Cathy convinced me to join the one thousand dollar rounds even though I was a little reluctant at first. But I am glad I did. Now I had to come up with a plan to raise one thousand dollars every month to give to the next team member and thank God for his faithfulness; I never missed a month.

I drove uber to raise money. I also did extra hours as a home health aide, and each time God provided. It's amazing what

10. TESTIMONIES OF MIRACLES AFTER WORKING TALENTS

God can do if one has a willing heart. That year I managed to raise twelve thousand dollars to my surprise. One thing I know for sure is each time I worked Talents God did something different, but this time it was different. He not only blessed me financially but blessed me with a Husband during Talents. For me getting married was not an easy task due to generational evil spirits that were fighting me. Most of my Relationships failed before marriage proposal even if there was a proposal something would happen to stop it from going further and I was now in my mid-thirties. Two months before Talents were closed, I met my husband. Glory to God!!

I still remember it like yesterday when Dr Cathy used to say in a song in our WhatsApp chat, "These Talents are going to give you a husband" and for sure my husband came the same year. Oh, how I am grateful to God for opening my eyes about Talents. God has literally changed my name from Ms Sithole Musiwa to Mrs Flores because of Talents.

MIRACLES OF MARRIAGE AND A BETTER JOB
Elders Trove and Martha Khama-Orlando, USA

I first met Pastor Cathy in 2011 when she had visited the United States and within the short time, I spent with her I immediately knew in my spirit I had met a true woman of God.

Soon after she left the USA, I heard the wonderful news that they were going to be transferred to the USA in Dallas Texas, But they were still waiting for their visas and work permits.

When I spoke to her over the phone, I told her that "I am truly believing in my spirit that when you arrive here you are going to land with my husband."

While I was waiting for their transfer and because of my faith she introduced me to 21 days of praying and fasting and she also told me to change my measure of giving. I remember spending 30 days sleeping at the church praying and fasting and also, I changed my measure of giving, I remember giving about $3000 to the church and also ministered the male and female pastors at our church.

When they arrived in Dallas Texas in deed they arrived /landed with my husband, She had with her a photo of my now husband Trove Khama, and it was soon after those 21 days of praying and fasting.

We got married in 3 months soon after we had been introduced and now happily married for 5 years.

The following year was a year of working talents and I remember I had lost my job at the Bank of America and was now working as a senior care giver which we referred to as doing RRPP and making only about $25,000 to $30,000 a year Which was regarded as living under poverty according to USA standards. But because of what she had imparted in me when she encouraged me to join the $500 a month round, I immediately jumped into it and we worked about $5,000 that year of which to us it felt like we had worked $50,000 because of our financial situation.

Soon after that we had big breakthrough and indeed, we truly serve a faithful God, I did a certification in business intelligence and got an interview soon after that with one of the biggest companies in the world Deloitte and I was also going to be earning triple the amount I was making before. We also bought an 18-Wheeler truck soon after that and how we did it only God knows.

Since then our lives have changed so much and we have even started a business for taking care of seniors called Quality

10. TESTIMONIES OF MIRACLES AFTER WORKING TALENTS

Homecare Professionals and it's all because of giving in a "changed measure" way.

This year we are working talents again with a changed measure in mind and we've even joined a $1,000 a month around and we are just believing in God that He will give us the grace.

MIRACLES OF SOWING AND REAPING 100-FOLD Testimony
Elder Abigail Mugutso- New York USA.

I want to thank God for the opportunity to work Talents. Whenever there is a call or opportunity to work in the house of God, I have always wanted to be a partaker of the blessing.

Because of that obedience and desire, Me and my husband Denmark Mugutso have been working talents ever since we joined the church. From 2006 to 2011 I was working amounts ranging from $1,000 to $2,000. However, after Dr Cathy shared on Talents in 2011 while on a missionary trip from New Zealand, I was encouraged to break my alabaster box. In 2012 My husband and I sold the only property we had in Zimbabwe, a 4,000 square meter stand. We gave all the proceeds towards the Mbuya Dorcas talents.

However fast forward in 2016 when the ZEGU Miracle Talents were launched, I had an office day job and needed to do something extra to work these Talents. I worked what we call (RRPP), which means Rese, Rese, pese, pese, in Shona, but in English any general job . After my office job I would go for the overnight job in the health field . In a week I would work ranging 3 nights to 5 nights. After overnight shift freshen up and go to my office job.

From working this and other projects my husband and I

managed to work US$ 15,065, When I look back, I still do not understand How I pulled through the overnights then straight to day job.

Many miracles happened after that, but one notable one is that God repaid the stand we had sold for previous Talents by allowing us to buy a 46-hectare farm in Zimbabwe. The size of the farm is more than 100 times the size of the stand we sold for talents. Glory to God He is faithful.

There are many miracles that happened in my life after that because of working Talents including my husband's job paying for a business trip to go to the Holy Land the same dates that our church was going on a Pilgrims tour. So all his expenses and part of mine where paid for when we went for the Holy Land tour 2018 Pilgrims.

My testimony is mainly to encourage those who are not yet in business, you can still do something for the Lord. I have a good job and my husband too, but I sacrificed to do a general job so that I can raise money for Talents. Through working Talents, our lives have changed, we are experiencing a financial blessing.

I also do the same for home Talents and it has helped us to accomplish a lot of things we would not have accomplished if it was not for home Talents. School of Talents has taught me to be a hard-working woman, knowing very well that there is always profit in hard work.

I also know that to be alive and well together with my family, it's through working for God in Talents and other works. I have also realized that one must not decrease in giving or working for God but keep increasing so God's blessing can increase in one's life. I have also leant I must continue to be faithful with tithes whilst working Talents for God to continue blessing me. Amen

10. TESTIMONIES OF MIRACLES AFTER WORKING TALENTS

MIRACLES OF DOMINATING THE DOLLAR
Pastors Dumisani and Coleen Mawoyo -Dallas, Texas, USA

The school of talents has taught us so many things .We have learned that if you lay aside all your desires and put God first by working for Him, He is Faithful and He will reward you. We have been working talents ever since God called us in the ministry. God blessed our businesses and at one point we were able to give an ambulance to the Mbuya Dorcas hospital in Zimbabwe which was one of the first ambulances used there. We did not stop there in 2014 we worked close to US $40K and our lives have never been the same since then. We have seen uncommon favor in the marketplace, growth in business and just supernatural provision in our lives. Our trucking businesses increased from two trucks to a fleet of 6 trucks in a short space of time. In 2016 God blessed us with twins, two wonderful boys Shawn and Shane despite the doctors saying we were not able to have children. God birthed another business this 2018 which is a Home-care business and my wife who is a nurse by profession has not gone back to work as she is running the business , what started as one home has tripled and all in one year. God has taught us not to be dominated by the USD but to dominate it.

MIRACLES OF MAKING THE DOLLAR CHEAP Talents testimony by
Deacon Julie Chitiyo -New York, USA

It all started in 2015; I was a new believer who didn't understand what working talents meant. I remember Dr Cathy came to our Easter conference and our entire region had raised only $1,000. I remember her saying, and I quote "the whole region is on this

$1000 and we are 4 months in already. Even the Chairing Elders are in that $1000?" then she chuckled. I wasn't able to go to that conference, but it was being recorded live and I was watching it from home. Her message that day on working talents stirred me so much I couldn't even sleep that night wondering how I could also work talents and work for God. I ordered her book "Change your measure" and that book stirred me up even more. The truth is, money from our paychecks is not enough to work talents, one has to start a side project/business and use that money for talents. With that in mind, I decided to start a cleaning business and I signed up as a franchisee. That year I worked $15,000! Our $1,000 ended up being over $100,000 for the region! The good thing is when the talents are done, money from that business goes into my pocket and helps my family. My business has been blessed, I now employ 3 couples and we service doctors' offices, Realtor offices including Urgent Care facilities. We have had customers requesting our team specifically for their properties to the point that some offices called to ask us how we manage our service and they wanted us to help train other teams. It's just The Lord's grace. Dr Cathy always used to say don't worship the dollar…make the dollar cheap and that's exactly what I have done. All you need is a willing heart and the Lord will do the rest. We thank God for the servant & Apostle and the vision of Talents.

MIRACLES OF NEW BUSINESS OPPORTUNITIES
Pfungwa and Tabetha Sikereta -Auckland, New Zealand.

We worked in Obedience to the word that was given to our father the Servant and Apostle of God Professor Ezekiel H.Guti. As we obeyed the word of God that was being taught on working Talents, our Spirits were quickened, and God opened doors for

10. TESTIMONIES OF MIRACLES AFTER WORKING TALENTS

us to work ZEGU Talents. The Holy Spirit impressed on hearts this word from 1 Chronicles 29:14 and we worked and worked and were faithful to give God the money. In the whole nation of New Zealand, we were Number 2 and worked a total of around $44000 together with our two children. We have continued to support our father in Missions as God has been Ministering to us as a family to support him whenever he goes to new nations. Our God is faithful. We have seen that if you obey the word of God, God will surely reward you. After working Talents, God has blessed us with businesses here in New Zealand and we continue to see His Grace in our lives.

"God has blessed us with a Steam Boilers operation training & Compliance Certification business and an Engineering Contracting business."

MIRACLES OF BUSINESS OPPORTUNITIES
DEREK AND TANAKA SHONHIWA -BOSTON, USA

We were new in the church when talents were called for in 2016. We were obedient and heeded the call. As taught by the Overseers we had to look for a way to raise finances other that what we were currently doing. We started to pray for God to make a way. A friend with a medical transportation business without asking, promised us if we bought a van from a friend of his, who was in vehicle sales, would run it for us in their business and give us the proceeds. This could only have been God, because we literally had to do nothing the whole time and raised over $23,000 through this opportunity. At the persistence of our friend, two years later we decided to look further into this business and realized the potential and after about six months of setting up, the business is fully licensed and operating and generating more revenue than we anticipated. This all because of talents.

During the time of Talents, we were also believing and trusting God to help us with our healthcare business, though it took a while, the scope has grown to more than our initial expectations. Another idea that came about during talents, though still in it's infancy, we also now have an independently owned real estate business and are looking at franchising out. God has really been showing His hand in our lives. We are amazed at the heights that he has been bringing us and we anticipate doing a lot more in His Kingdom because we believe that is where our breakthroughs are.

DELIVERANCE FROM SPIRIT OF LACK TO ABUNDANCE
Elders Dominic and Peace Maminingu -Polonkwane, South Africa

The school of talents has changed our lives from a life of lack to abundance, from renting to being landlords. God gave us grace in 2016 when we worked Zegu miracle talents as a family. The hunger to participate started in December 2015 when our Overseers came and told the church that 2016 was declared Zegu miracle talents year. We did what we called "vhura muromo" meaning we were to give something to show we were starting to work talents. We didn't want to start small, so we gave big, R30000. As the year progressed God opened many doors for us in the area of construction. We committed to say every job we will get we will give everything to Zegu

We saw Isaiah 1:19 working for us; if you are willing and obedient you will eat the good of the land.

10. TESTIMONIES OF MIRACLES AFTER WORKING TALENTS

I remember one time the payment was late and when it came the big day was just around the corner. We needed groceries for the house but the passion to participate made us to give everything that we had. It was when we got home that we started seeing there was no food in the house. We only had a packet of mealie meal and a bag full of Kapenta(small dried fish).

That's the food that took us through that whole month and we didn't see how the month passed because of the joy we felt knowing that we are giving a God who gives back a good measure, pressed down, shaken together and running over.

We got contracts for road and housing construction, and boreholes

It brought us so much joy to partner with the servants of God and by the time talents were finished we had managed to raise over 786 000 Rands equivalent to $55000(USD)

From 2016 up until now we have seen our lives changing. God is abundantly blessing and changing our lifestyle. We have managed to acquire 4 properties. 2 in Zimbabwe and 2 in South Africa, of which one is business warehouse . We cannot talk of cars. Since then we have driven all types of cars to the latest Mercedes Benz. All this through the blessings coming from working for our God.

Our company is still growing and reaching more areas in South Africa.

We are truly thankful to the Servant and Apostles of God our father and mother Apostle E H Guti and Dr Eunor Guti for bringing such a school which powerfully changes lives.

MIRACLES OF BIG BUSINESS CONTRACTS
Elders Mendy and Sgauke -Polonkwane, South Africa

In 2015 we managed to raise funds for Zegu through sub contracts as Insig construction. The company had no experience, lack of capacity and funding. We also got funds from the sales from our small shop we were renting in town. Even though we had funds from these businesses we felt that we needed to go an extra mile ,so we started cleaning people's houses to raise more funds for Zegu…God gave us the grace to work R144000 Rands. To us it was a miracle because our monthly revenue was R10000 and our monthly expenses were more than the salaries.

After working these miracle talents God opened our eyes to change Insig construction to an engineering company. For years we were bidding for tenders but not getting anything to the extent that we almost lost hope. But because of working sacrificially for God through talents a miracle happened in 2018 we were awarded a tender worthy millions which was supposed to be awarded to ten companies. Even though our company had no experience .God Blessed us again we opened 2 big boutiques in town with top class clothes from Turkey and China .We are getting more projects and God has raised our standard as a family.

Talents Oh Yeah!!!!

MIRACLE OF GETTING A JOB IN USA FEDERAL GOVERNMENT
Elder Bertha Nhemwa -Maryland, USA

I want to thank the God of Ezekiel for working Talents. I don't own a business, but I have a regular job. I worked talents by preparing taxes for people and I was doing a monthly round with some believers in our Assembly. When I was working talents, I applied for a job with the local government. It is very hard to get a job in the local government if you don't know anyone. But

10. TESTIMONIES OF MIRACLES AFTER WORKING TALENTS

I applied all the same and I got the job. I worked for 4 and half years and we got a new director who didn't like me, and I was having a rough time with her, so I started looking for another job. That year I worked talents for $5,500. Getting a job in the local government is not easy and worse still is in the federal, I believed in God and I applied for a federal job.

I was called for an interview on Friday and the following Monday they started calling my references. Within a week I was made an offer. The offer was less than I was getting by $8000 but I told the HR lady that I can't accept because the salary was much lower than what I was getting. The recruiter told me to just accept the offer and then negotiate. So, I accepted the offer with a request to negotiate my salary. I told them how much I was getting and asked if they could at least match what I was getting. They requested my last 2 paychecks and I sent them.

They accepted my request and made me a new offer. When I started the job, they gave me $3,000 more than I was getting in the local government. It takes 6 months to one year before an offer is made in federal but for me it took 2 weeks and I had to give a 2-day notice that I was quitting because the federal wanted to me start the following Monday. To God be the glory.

Godfrey and Ethel Mutara - United Kingdom.

It was on a long awaited big Sunday in 1996 in a small area in Filabusi, a tiny but developing town in Matebeleland South province in Zimbabwe. The church was packed to capacity.

Our Provincial Overseers David and Emma Gangata were guest speakers.

It was when Overseer Emma Gangata was preaching on the school of talents and the working of talents that she suddenly pointed to my wife Ethel Mutara and she said, "I mean you, you mai Mutara; I want you to start working talents, Your nursing profession is not enough"

She was speaking with an authoritative voice and boldness of speech. It was evident that she was under a great annoiting of the Spirit of God.

Something unexplainable happened within our hearts as Overseer Emma Gangata laid hands and prayed for us at the end of the session. From this day forth we have obeyed and have never looked back as we knew that great deliverance had taken place.

Giving to the work of the kingdom, working of talents and prayer has not been an easy sailing. We have been and we are faithful tithers and we support the work of God financially.

Our first business venture was a small grocery shop (commonly referred to as tuckshop in Zimbabwe) in Bindura, Zimbabwe. Business mistakes were made and lesons learnt.

Now based in the United Kingdom, Leicester in England, in 2006 we established a health and social care company which has done so well even during the great CREDIT CRUNCH of 2008 and 2009 with an annual turnover of £680.000.

Through this business we have supported the work of God in working of talents and notably the construction of a church building in the rural area of Mudzimirema, Marondera in Zimbabwe. This building is at the very site which is written in the book The History of ZAOGA FIF, The book of Rememberance, Where it is going and where it came from.

10. TESTIMONIES OF MIRACLES AFTER WORKING TALENTS

We now running a Health and social care training business and a property investment business.

Having been born and grew up in a rural background and from a poor background with no history of business ownership in the family, it is amazing that God has gone such great works through obedience, giving and the working of talent.

Truly God will not put to shame those that believe in Him.

Roman 10: 11
For the Scripture says, "Whoever believes on Him will not be put to shame."

MIRACLES OF RELOCATION
Elder Violet Mashingaidze - Nashville Tennesse.

My history on Talents starts right back from Zimbabwe. I was selling Zimbabwe's staple food for Talents. Sadza and either beef, chicken, or sausages, with veggies, for lunch in the industrial sites of Harare. After Talents I continued and was supplementing my family income.

God indeed rewarded me. Miracles followed me after Talents. One of the miracles is that me and my family relocated to the United States of America, me first then shortly afterwards my family joined me. After getting the opportunity to go to USA, that sadza money paid for my air ticket.

Even being in the USA, I didn't drop the ball. The last time we worked Talents, I was crocheting dish towels for sell. I had acquired a skill in crotchet work as a young girl. By putting it to work, I worked Talents.

In working Talents, you have to look with spiritual eyes. Look at what you have, in terms of skills, knowledge, and competence. Don't concentrate on what you don't have.

While in the USA, God continued to reward me. I went back to school and I am now a nurse, a profession I had desired from childhood. I also own a beautiful 3 bedroomed home, on split levels, with a large basement. All this in a nice, up-kept neighborhood. By the way, I also drive a debt free car. This had to be the hand of God.

Conclusion

It is grace to be allowed to work Talents. I pray that the Lord will open the eyes of every person who reads this book so that they can also unlock their miracles through working Talents.

May the Lord open your heart and stir you up to good works.

Stay blessed,

Dr Cathy

You can reach Dr. Cathy on cmarambakuyana@yahoo.co.nz

Made in the USA
Middletown, DE
18 March 2022